# BROADWAY DOWN EAST:

## AN INFORMAL ACCOUNT OF THE PLAYS, PLAYERS AND PLAYHOUSES OF BOSTON FROM PURITAN TIMES TO THE PRESENT

## BY ELLIOT NORTON

Lectures Delivered for the

National Endowment for the Humanities

Boston Public Library Learning Library Program

Boston, Trustees of the Public Library of the City of Boston, 1978

**Library of Congress Cataloging in Publication Data**

PN2277.B       792′09744′61       78-7004

ISBN 0-89073-055-5

Norton, Elliot, 1903-
  Broadway down east.


(Publication—National Endowment for the
Humanities Learning Library Program, Boston Public
Library ; 5)
  Bibliography: p.
  Includes index.
  1. Theater—Massachusetts—Boston—History—
Addresses, essays, lectures. 2. Boston—History.
I. Title. II Series: Boston. Public Library.
National Endowment for the Humanities Learning
Library Program. Publication—National Endowment
for the Humanities Learning Library Program ; 5.

# BROADWAY DOWN EAST

# TABLE OF CONTENTS

# INTRODUCTION

This book is based on lectures given at the Boston Public Library during a period of eight weeks beginning April 7, 1977, designed to trace informally, but with as much accuracy as I could muster, the history of the theater in Boston from the earliest years to the present time. The lectures were made possible by the National Endowment for the Humanities (NEH), as part of a vital project under which the library was designated as a "learning library" and entrusted with educating the general public without cost in subjects or disciplines that needed to be explored, or cultivated, by Bostonians of good will, of whom there are many, and intellectual curiosity, of whom there are still quite a few.

Since there had been no "Record of the Boston Stage" since William W. Clapp, Jr.'s book of that title (1853), and since the theater has been notably, if peculiarly, active in our city of "Bibles, Brahmins, and Bosses" since that time, and since I have been deeply involved during the last forty years as drama critic, lecturer, and teacher, Philip J. McNiff, director of the library, invited me to marshal the available facts, to present them orally, then in writing.

It became apparent during the first few weeks of research, as it had been to Mr. McNiff all along, that a definitive history would be impossible, and perhaps not even desirable under the circumstances. The subject is too vast, and many of the details would be of little interest to theatergoers, whose concern, we all hoped, was for a broad picture of what had happened, who had been responsible, and why we have the kind of theater we have now in our City on a Hill.

With the concurrence of Mr. McNiff and of Paul M. Wright, head of the Learning Library Program, I elected to cover the subject by considering several broad topics, each as a whole, instead of traversing it year by year. After an initial lecture that set down some of the occasionally peculiar attitudes of the founding and following fathers to the theater and to people of the stage, I discussed in sequence the story of Boston's playhouses; the record of actors and actresses—first the English, then the continentals and the native Americans—an account of the resident acting troupes from the eighteenth-century stock companies to the present regional and "fringe" players; then the history and the hazards of the tryout system, which is basic in Boston; the censorship, which is peculiar; and, finally, the present situation.

To develop and expand on my own contributions, I invited Douglass Shand Tucci, architectural historian; Professor Sherwood Collins of Tufts University; Michael J. Murray, former director of the Charles Playhouse Company and present artistic director of the Cincinnati Playhouse-in-the-Park; and Richard J. Sinnott, Chief of the Licensing Division in the office of the mayor of Boston, and in effect "last of the city censors," to speak, each on his specialty. They did; to each, for his contribution, I am grateful.

Some of the lectures have been amplified for publication. In addition, I have supplied appendixes identifying some of the principal playhouses of Boston, and giving statistics on long runs of plays and musicals. Paul Wright has made possible a map to indicate where the major theaters are, or have been.

I am grateful to Philip McNiff, to Paul Wright, and, for extraordinary assistance in research without which the lectures and the book would not have been possible, to Y. T. Feng, assistant director of the Boston Public Library, and especially to Diana Kleiner of her staff.

ELLIOT NORTON

# BROADWAY DOWN EAST

# CHAPTER I

## THE NIGHT THEY RAIDED 'ROMEO AND JULIET'

There is a great scene in Shakespeare's loveliest romantic comedy, "Twelfth Night," in which the drunken Sir Toby Belch and his foolish companion, Sir Andrew Aguecheek, having been reprimanded and discomfited by the steward Malvolio, are sputtering their indignation, trying to find a word to fit his wickedness and to solace their battered pride. The Lady Olivia's maid, Maria, helps them in their search for an appropriate epithet by suggesting that sometimes Malvolio is "a kind of Puritan," to which silly Sir Andrew replies indignantly, "Oh, if I thought that, I'd beat him like a dog!" Sir Toby wonders what "exquisite" reason his chum might have for that kind of violence, but Andrew is only sputtering; he has no "exquisite" reason, but he has "good reason enough."

The probability is that Andrew was uttering the general feeling of Elizabethan players and playgoers against the Puritans, who at that time, about 1600, had a good deal of political clout in London and who, when they eventually came to control England in the time of Cromwell, closed down every theater in London. There were many sects of Puritans, but they were all obsessed with a sense of sin and all convinced that the theater was a steaming cauldron of lewdness.

It was the members of one of these sects who in 1630, twenty-nine years after Malvolio first made his threat, founded the city of Boston as a haven where they could live in peace and prosper according to their own ideals. They were, by and large, good people, and in some cases heroic people; if their code of morals was strict, they adhered to it strictly. They were also bigoted, narrow-minded,

*opposite: Howard Athenaeum (1845-1962), Howard Street.*

and intolerant of anyone whose views differed from theirs.

Some of their descendants stood up to the British muskets at Concord and Lexington and helped make the American Revolution. Others, later on, protected William Lloyd Garrison when he began his battle against slavery; it was from nearby Concord where he was sheltered that John Brown set out on his raid on Harper's Ferry. In the meantime, however, the founding fathers of Boston had banished Roger Williams to the wilderness for daring to disagree with their religious prescriptions, and two years later, in 1638, had done the same thing to Anne Hutchinson.

One hundred and twenty years after the first of these formidable people sailed in a fleet of eleven ships into Boston Harbor, some young men of Boston got the idea that it would be nice to put on a play in a coffeehouse: nothing wicked, just a modest production of Thomas Otway's play, "The Orphan." So many people tried to get in, the story goes, that the legislature, acting with a celerity that would startle our present members of the Great and General Court, immediately passed a law forbidding all stage plays as "tending to increase immorality, impiety and a contempt of religion" and imposing fines not only on managers but on actors and even on playgoers.

It was forty-seven years before that law was repealed, and more than a century later some church groups were still fighting the theater as a wicked institution, and not only in sermons.

Boston was not alone in this hostility to the acted drama. Although Williamsburg in Virginia had had a playhouse since 1718 and New York as early as 1730, there was a general feeling in many of the colonies that playhouses were places of potential

corruption. But the hostility was more intense, more bitter here, and while it subsided some in the nineteenth century as certain descendants of the Puritans abandoned, or relaxed, their religious convictions, it was continued by some of the newer sects, and when they and later the Irish immigrants began to take over political power, it emerged anew in the form of an official censorship of books and plays so uncompromising that the common phrase "banned in Boston" became a national joke, or a national scandal, depending on which way you looked at it.

Forty-two years after the legislature banned plays and actors as a danger to the town, a company of English actors began presenting such plays as "Othello" and "Romeo and Juliet" under the guise of "moral lectures," in a makeshift theater on Board Alley (now Hawley Street). The theater manager was arrested by a sheriff and brought to Faneuil Hall for a hearing. He was released, and the theater was free to put on such other moral lectures as "The Contrast," by Royall Tyler, a former Bostonian who had left town after John Adams refused to consent to Tyler's marriage to his daughter, Abby.

Two years later, with substantial citizens furnishing the funds and with Charles Bulfinch as architect, the first real playhouse was built on Federal Street, at the corner of Franklin, and from that time on drama has had a home in Boston.

Conflict is, by general consensus, the essence, the soul, of drama. In Boston, conflict has been a way of life for those who have dared to love and those who have lived to hate the theater. All down through the years, there have been forces within the community favoring the theater at its fullest and freest, and others, often just as passionate, straining to keep it down, or even to close it down. During those years, the battle of the proponents and creators of drama has been for freedom to say what they had to say, without let or hindrance. The struggle of the actors, as proud professionals, has been for respectability and full acceptance.

It will sound scandalous, but it is pretty well established that John Hancock, then governor of

Massachusetts, instigated the raid on the New Exhibition Room, that first theater in Boston. At any rate the patrons thought so, and the records show they trampled a picture of him that was on display. We know, too, that Sam Adams, another American hero, was also hostile to the theater, and that is sad. We like to think of those whom we admire as being altogether wise and humane and, in such cases as these, full of our own wisdom about the nature and the grandeur of the theater. That Hancock and Adams were not does not lessen our admiration for their political courage, but it hurts just the same.

Just as disturbing, and perhaps more to the point, is the story that on the night they raided "Romeo and Juliet," a gang of toughs appeared at Hancock's house, full of the news and probably full of other stimulants too, told him they had heard of the arrests, and urged that he order them to go down to Board Alley and tear down the New Exhibition Room; since the theater had been improvised from an abandoned stable, they could easily have done it. To Hancock's credit, he insisted they refrain from razing the Augean stable; to theirs, they heeded him. What is interesting, I think, is that the feeling for and against the theater was not confined to clergy nor to the upper ranks of Boston society. The audience was obviously middle or lower class, else they would not have raised as much hell as they did, and the gang who offered to throw that building down were surely not Brahminical.

That's the way it has been through the years in Boston, though the leaders of the opposition, the enemy, have generally been of the middle class. In many cases, these captains of the battalia have been clergymen of various denominations. For the Puritans, though they began to lose their rigid hold on their followers—some of whom, having made a little or a lot of money, turned to gayer ways of life—gave way to other sects who have followed the Puritan line.

One of the newer groups who looked on the theater with alarm was the Baptists, whom the Puritans hated, but who got into Boston in 1679

by way of Charlestown. That they should have a church here represented some kind of primary justice, for they were in a way spiritual heirs of Roger Williams. He had been a free spirit; they were not always. . . .

In 1843, having grown in number and influence, the members of the Reverend Mr. Colver's Baptist Society bought the Tremont Theater on Tremont Street, closed it down, and made it over into Tremont Temple, on the same site where the present temple stands.

The Tremont had been one of the successful theaters of Boston, flourishing when the playhouse on Federal Street was running downhill. But it,

too, had been losing money. So the Baptists bought it and made it their headquarters. The presumption is that they took it over because it was a good central location, suited to their needs, and that may be the simple truth. Theater people didn't believe it.

W. W. Clapp, Jr., the first historian of the Boston stage, writing in 1853, reported that when the manager of the theater, J. S. Jones, came forward on the Tremont stage to address the final night's audience, "he did not enlarge on the causes that will transform the theater into another institution." But if he had chosen to do that, "he could do so, and show that they did not originate so much in a desire for private and public good, as in the un-

*The first Boston Theater, on Federal Street at Franklin (also called Federal Street Theater) designed by Charles Bulfinch, opened 1794, destroyed by fire and rebuilt four years later, razed in 1852 and supplanted two years later by the grand new Boston Theater which stood on Washington Street (where the Sack Savoy is now) until 1925.*

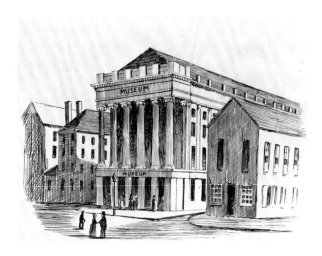

*The original Boston Museum, opened in 1841 on Tremont at Bromfield Street, closed in 1846 when a new Museum was built farther down Tremont, next to King's Chapel Burying Ground.*

worthy motive to subserve the base designs of aversion and bigotry.''

In other, perhaps simpler words, Clapp, the editor of the *Boston Evening Gazette*, was insinuating that the Baptists bought the theater in order to put it out of business, just because it was a theater. Whether that insinuation was justified, I do not profess to know, but the fact that it could be made in print by a conservative and influential Bostonian indicates that the old tensions were there.

At the same time that the Tremont Theater gave way to Tremont Temple, another playhouse was flourishing a block away, on Tremont Street at the corner of Bromfield. The Boston Museum, as it was called, had been opened in 1841 as a museum displaying not only paintings but stuffed animals on the first floor, with concerts in a hall upstairs. In 1843, the concerts gave way to performances of plays which became so successful that a new Boston Museum was built farther down Tremont Street, alongside the King's Chapel Burying Ground, three years later.

This new Boston Museum flourished within a block of Tremont Temple, and continued until 1903

as one of Boston's great theaters. That it was called a museum is pertinent to my thesis. It is a matter of record that the hostility to the theater was so great that many proper Bostonians refused to go to a playhouse, but being naive, shall we say, they would allow themselves to be seen in a museum.

If this seems fanciful today, consider the testimony of Kate Ryan, who was a member of the Boston Museum stock company for twenty years. Writing in 1915, Kate referred to the famous old theater as ''a meeting place where those who did not wish to be regarded as theatregoers could visit without a blush. Many of the regular habitués of the Boston Museum, even after it had become much more of a theater, fondly believed they were not attending a regular playhouse.'' Do we call that naiveté or by a harsher term, as, for instance, hypocrisy? In either case, it is plain evidence that even on the verge of the twentieth century, there were Bostonians whose prejudices against ''regular playhouses'' ran strong and deep.

The Baptists put up with the Boston Museum and with the new Howard Athenaeum, which was only two blocks away, at least for awhile. In the meantime, the Methodists had taken up the old Puritan plaint against theaters, and not just against specific plays, or moral offense, but against the theater as an institution.

On March 15, 1863, just around the corner from Tremont Temple, the pastor of the Bromfield Street Methodist Church preached a sermon against the theater which was subsequently published in pamphlet form and which might have been uttered by one of the old Puritan divines. ''The theater,'' he thundered, ''is a house of pleasure, or amusement, and not of recreation . . . ,'' and ''this discourse is not directed against any abuse of the institution, but against the institution itself . . . against this, its central idea, we protest in the name of all that is good and true.''

That, in 1863, in the Athens of America. . . .

Thirteen years later, the Baptists of Tremont Temple and some of their Methodist and Episcopal colleagues got together to form the Watch and Ward Society, which set itself up as a guardian of

public morality in literature and eventually in the theater, keeping alive well into the twentieth century the Puritan conscience with vigorous, direct action.

The Watch and Ward had its biggest successes in the period between 1913 and 1926 when, under its prompting, booksellers and some of the Boston newspapers joined with its leaders to see to it that books the society considered immoral were kept out of the bookstores. During those years, a committee of three Watchers and Warders and an equal number of booksellers screened all books that might perhaps seem offensive and saw to it that all stores were warned against selling or displaying them. The newspapers cooperated by not accepting their advertising and by not reviewing them.

Before that arrangement ended in 1926, the Watch and Ward had begun to meddle with theaters, too, selecting the Howard Athenaeum for special attention. The Howard had opened in 1845 as a center of culture, presenting the great acting companies and opera troupes. But these gave way to variety shows of little distinction. About 1880, the public began to call the playhouse, more or less affectionately, the "Old Howard," and when in the twenties the managers chose to put on burlesque shows that stripped its comics of decency and its ladies of their clothes, the Watch and Ward watched and warded some of its performers into municipal court.

In the meantime, Boston had acquired a city censor for plays and movies, and for the Old Howard, too. In 1904, Mayor Patrick Collins appointed a former musician named John M.

*Grand Staircase of the Boston Museum.*

*Grand Promenade of the Boston Museum.*

*The Boston Museum (1846-1903) in a sketch made in 1853 that indicates its location at 18 Tremont Street (present Kimball Building) next to King's Chapel Burying Ground.*

Casey as a messenger in his office, because Casey could no longer play the kettledrums and now needed a job, and because his father and Pat Collins were friends. Presently, Collins promoted John Casey to be head of the city division that licensed theaters, and John went out to warn away all plays, all musicals, all acts and actors whose work might jeopardize the morals of Bostonians. In the twenty-eight years before he retired, he had successfully urged the managers of hundreds of plays and musicals to alter their texts, or their costumes, to conform to Boston law in ways that I will consider in more detail on subsequent pages.

During all this period Boston had, of course, been growing from a small town on the end of a peninsula to a city of 600,000 spread over many acres, some of which—like the site of the Public Library—were made of land reclaimed by fill from the waters of what was literally the "Back Bay."

The new Bostonians were immigrants. Many who arrived in the period after the potato famine in the 1840s were Irish. They had no truck with the Puritans, or their successors, who disliked them too. But in matters of sexual morality they were more Puritan than the original settlers. Or, as the Reverend Frank Chase, the Methodist minister who was head of the Watch and Ward Society, said with a smile in a 1925 interview, "The Irish make good Puritans."

The Irish didn't go to the theater much, but because they controlled City Hall in the twenties they supported the censorship of plays and, by indirection, of books, too. One commentator suggested that part of the power of the Watch and Ward lay in the probability that if any author or publisher dared go to court to fight one of their rulings, the jury would be predominantly Irish and Catholic, and would very likely stand with the Baptists and Methodists. At this point, it may be

*Exterior of the Boston Theater on Washington Street, opened in 1854. Seating 3000, it was one of the great playhouses of the country and served as our opera house until the Boston Opera House was built in 1909. It was razed in 1925 to make way for the B. F. Keith Memorial Theater, which later became the Sack Savoy.*

worth pointing out that the idea that books and the theater should be purified was held not merely by Methodists, Baptists, and the newly arrived Catholics, but by many members of the old aristocracy and the intelligentsia, who supported the Watch and Ward with their words, and their contributions, too.

Book censorship began to break down as the times changed in 1926. Stage censorship had already been weakened, technically at least, in 1915 by a statute that divided power to close theaters among members of a committee of three. Actually, plays were banned, or at least warned against coming to Boston, or in some cases had alterations thrust upon them, until 1961, when the

Civil Liberties Union fought the censors over alterations in "Who's Afraid of Virginia Woolf?" A changing moral climate, the new permissiveness, and new judicial decisions about the nature of obscenity helped to diminish the power of the censors, but it was not until 1975, two hundred years after Lexington and Concord, that full freedom of expression on the stage was achieved. "Equus," by Peter Shaffer, which opened at the Wilbur Theater on November 18, 1975, violated most of the precepts that John M. Casey had held as inviolable standards, but it was not censored, nor was it threatened. In a new climate of free expression, this was a breakthrough.

In the meantime, actors and actresses had been

*Playbill for George Frederick Cooke's appearance in 1812 at the Federal Street (Boston) Theater. He was the first in a long line of English stars to play here.*

stars from time to time, including all the great ones of the world. They presented contemporary plays, the classic dramas of Shakespeare, sometimes opera, occasionally "variety."

Toward the end of the nineteenth century the pattern began to change, as stars of greater or less repute put together entire productions and toured with them across the country, playing Boston, of course, and every other city, small and large. For fifty years, we had in Boston a mix of local acting companies and touring troupes. Then, in the 1920s, a number of things happened that shook up the entire apparatus of the American theater. After that the American theater faced New York as the hub and center of everything.

The revolution began when the movies came of age in 1915; it was intensified by the restrictions of World War I, which made it difficult for theater companies to travel, exacerbated by the addition of sound to the silent films, by the beginnings in 1926 of national radio, and pushed into a second violent phase in 1948, when television, for better or worse, became a national institution.

In 1915, there were fifteen playhouses in Boston, four with resident professional stock companies. In 1932, the last of the stock companies, that run by E. E. Clive at the old Copley Theater, closed its doors. After that, the only way was that of Broadway, and we in Boston, like the playgoers of Philadelphia and such other eastern seaboard cities as New Haven, became ancillaries. We had a great symphony orchestra; that was ours. We had our art museum. We still had a Boston Opera House, though there was no opera company to play there except when the Metropolitan came in the spring. But our playhouses, now numbering seven, existed only to play Broadway shows, good or bad, and most of these were being prepared not for us but for the New York audience. We had, in other words, become a tryout town. We are today, despite some interesting efforts to give us back our own theatrical identity, just that: a city where plays and musicals are tested, prepared, often revised, and made ready, not for us but very often at our expense, for New York.

fighting their own battle for respectability and had won it largely because of the courage of a young woman of Boston, Charlotte Cushman. In an atmosphere of tension, of Puritan hostility on the one hand and something reasonably close to Dionysian enthusiasm on the other, the theater of Boston has not only continued to exist but has occasionally flourished, and has had its moments of glory.

In the beginning, our theaters followed the national pattern, which was based on the older customs of England. They had, that is to say, resident acting companies to which came visiting

## Howard Athenæum.

### HOWARD STREET.

## NEW MANAGEMENT

☞ This Beautiful Theatre is now in new hands. An excellent Company is engaged, an
eral distinguished Artistes will appear in succession.

E. BURTON, - - - - - - LESSEE AND DIRECTOF
J. BARTON, - - - - ACTING MANAGER AND TREASUREF
AGE MANAGER, - - - - MR. W. L. AYLING

### ☞ ALTERATION OF TIME ☜

#### DOORS OPEN AT 6 1-2,—TO BEGIN AT 7 O'CLOCK.

The Public are respectfully informed that the

## HREE REMAINING NIGHTS

### Of the Engagement of

# MR. MACREADY

### Will be this Wednesday, Thursday & Friday.

which occasion this INIMITABLE ARTISTE will appear in his most Popular Characters.

#### FIRST TIME IN BOSTON of the Celebrated Tragedy of

# KING LEAR !

### According to the Text of Shakspeare.

ing Lear, - - Mr Macready

#### SUPPORTED BY THE FULL STRENGTH OF THIS SPLENDID COMPANY.

## RS J. WALLACK AS GONERIL

| Mr. RYDER, | as | KENT, |
| Mr. LYNNE, | as | EDGAR, |
| Mr. Bowers, | as | Alabany, |
| Mr. Ayling, | as | Edmund, |
| MRS. FLYNN, | as | CORDELIA. |

### Cast which cannot be Equalled by any Theatre in the Union !

## Vednesday Evening, Nov. 8th, 1848.

#### Will be presented Shakspeares' Tragedy of

# KING LEAR!

### KING LEAR, - - MR. MACREADY

We have three fine playhouses—two of them, the Colonial and the Wilbur, among the best in the United States in all ways. We have an audience that has changed down through the years, and changes, as a matter of fact, from one type of production to the next, but that is still ready and willing to go to the theater even at today's extraordinarily high prices. We have won full freedom from censorship, and we have begun to develop since the closing of E. E. Clive's company at the Copley a growing network of smaller resident acting organizations, some of them transient, some of them terrible, a few, at least, adventurous and promising. We have survived a serious urban situation that for a time threatened the entire area of lower Tremont and Boylston streets, where our major theaters have been located since the beginning of the century.

All down through the years there have been sections of the city in which the laws and the conventions were exuberantly flaunted and the theaters menaced by improper Bostonians. In the nineteenth century one such district existed on the west side of Beacon Hill, where an estimated three hundred shady ladies annoyed the neighbors and frequented the theaters on Tremont Street and Howard Street. Later, when the Howard Athenaeum became a burlesque theater, with another called Waldron's Casino on nearby Hanover Street, the action moved into what was then Scollay Square and which has since become the chaste Government Center.

Ten years ago the Boston Redevelopment Authority (B.R.A.) tore down the Old Howard and the Casino and moved the ladies and their fellows into an area on Washington Street, to be bounded, so they said, by Essex and Stuart streets, where one of our most famous playhouses, the Globe, had presented some of our greatest stars; and half a block from the Park Theater, which had been a home of stars too, until the Minsky Brothers turned

*William Macready, one of England's superstars of the 19th century, played the Howard Athenaeum in 1848 in "King Lear."*

it into a burlesque house more noisome than the Howard had ever been. The B.R.A. insisted that this new section, this "adult entertainment zone," would carefully contain and restrain all the wicked ones among us; in it our sporty convention visitors would be safely, if evilly, entertained.

The trouble with that notion—or at least *one* trouble—is that this adult entertainment zone, which the public christened the Combat Zone, never was contained, and presently began to disgorge its ladies and their pimps, with hustlers and drug peddlers, into the area where our playhouses are located. When Mayor Kevin H. White was propositioned in the lobby of the Colonial Theater by one of a group of more picturesque hussies, some police relief was provided. But it took a grave protest by New York producers and theater owners to force municipal action.

The showmen came here as a delegation in 1975 to point out that unless they could get drastic relief so that their property, their playgoers, and their actors, too, would be protected, they would sell their theaters and go elsewhere. Since they were, and still are, plagued by a similar problem of even larger proportions in the Times Square area of New York, they knew the hazards. But they had some clout; their protests led to increased police protection, including the presence of mounted police in the area.

Sad to say, it took a murder to clean up the Combat Zone and to drive the predators off Tremont and Boylston streets. The killing of a Harvard football player, Andrew Puopolo, in 1976 created such a storm of protest that the section was saturated with police.

In the meantime, despite the hazards of the district, a new theater, the Charles Playhouse, had opened. Operated as a resident theater from 1957 till 1971, it is run now as a commercial theater for the presentation of plays and musicals from New York's Off Broadway and as such is important. Off Broadway has developed in the last twenty-five years a number of shows of interest to an audience more special than those of Broadway, and not really suitable for the Wilbur, the Colonial, or the Shubert. The best of these have a convenient home at the Charles.

Last year, one of the fifty little companies that have struggled for a foothold here since E. E. Clive left, the new Boston Repertory Theater, developed enough courage and a large enough mortgage to make possible a small but attractive playhouse within half a block of the Colonial, on Boylston Place. That gives us in our immediate downtown section, as of the spring of 1977, three big theaters capable of playing almost any show from New York or London, and two lesser ones, and if this is a somewhat less than perfect situation it is not, under the circumstances of today, bad. Not bad at all.

opposite: *National Theater, Portland and Traverse Streets (1832-1863).*

*Boston Opera House on Huntington Avenue, 1909-1957, served as home of Boston Opera Company and of the touring Metropolitan and other companies, also for musical comedies and plays with great stars. John Barrymore played there in "Hamlet"; Katharine Cornell in "Saint Joan." Razed to make way for a Northeastern University dormitory.*

# CHAPTER II

## PLEASURES AND PALACES: BULFINCH TO BLACKALL

In 1792, when a brave company of actors began producing their "moral lectures" in the New Exhibition Room, Boston was a small town on a peninsula ringed on three sides by water, connected to the rest of the world by a narrow isthmus that straggled along between mud flats on what is now Washington Street. Whether they liked the theater, as some did, or loathed it, Bostonians of that period were reasonably comfortable and content in their isolation. They did most of their business by water, and lived in homes that often had lovely gardens in an area bounded by the harbor, the Charles River—which spilled over into a great bay at the bottom of Boston Common—and the isthmus. There were eighteen thousand of them then, and although they had sharply different ideas on many subjects, they were generally homogeneous. The Congregational churches of the Puritans were soon to be supplanted in many places by those of the Unitarians. There were Baptists in town, too; Episcopalians and the Methodists would become powerful presently. But most Bostonians were of English descent and if they fought among themselves, as they sometimes did even in the streets, they had common roots.

By 1840, the tides of immigration had begun to flow, and presently there were thousands, then hundreds of thousands, of immigrants crowding into the North End. The town became a city in 1822 and, to make way for the newcomers, began to expand. One year before John Phillips took office as Boston's first mayor, commercial interests had built two dams in the Back Bay, intending to harness the water for mills. One of these projected out from the foot of Beacon Hill as a causeway, extending along Beacon Street to what is now

Kenmore Square; that gave a second access by land to Boston and led, in 1859, to the filling in of the Back Bay. In the meantime, four bridges had been thrust across the Charles River linking the city to Charlestown, Cambridge, and areas to the north.

The Public Garden was created in 1824 by Major Josiah Quincy on land opposite Boston Common. Then the waters beyond were filled with gravel and sand brought in from Needham on the new steam trains. In the last forty years of the nineteenth century the Back Bay began to take the shape it has today: Commonwealth Avenue, with its trees and shrubs, was thrust out in the direction of Brookline parallel to the dam road, which was now Beacon Street; Boylston Street was extended, and cross streets laid out in geometrical patterns. Trinity Church opened in Copley Square in 1871, and in 1895 the new Boston Public Library, which had been on Boylston Street where the Colonial Theater now stands, was erected on the opposite side.

The South End grew up on landfill dumped on either side of the isthmus leading to Roxbury and the world beyond. Early in the nineteenth century new streets were opened in this section, and Tremont, which had extended under two different names from where the Government Center now is as far as Boylston Street, was carried ahead into the new developments. Harrison Avenue, Shawmut Avenue, and Columbus Avenue were constructed parallel to Washington Street and Tremont, and the South End began to take shape. In the 1860s, the brick, bowfront houses that still exist in many places were built by real-estate speculators, who hoped to make this the fashion-

able residential area of the city. The speculation didn't work out for a number of reasons that only a realtor could understand. The Back Bay became fashionable, while the South End, except for a few pockets of handsome houses in streets like Union Park, became a rooming-house area where some of the thousands of immigrants lived.

As the Back Bay and the South End developed, merging finally into one great area divided only by railroad tracks and social taboos, some of the theaters began to move out, too. But only a few. Theaters always tend to hang together, for comfort, reassurance, and protection. They hang, and they huddle; at least, they do in Boston. In New York, the playhouses began way downtown and moved up as the city did. Here, they started near the center of town, which in 1792 was the old State House at the corner of what are now Washington and State streets, and stayed there for a long time.

Douglass Tucci's monograph, "The Boston Rialto: Playhouses, Concert Halls, and Movie Palaces," published in January 1977, takes the form of an escorted tour around the district in which the old theaters were and the present ones are. It is interesting to realize that this is a walking tour, that the old playhouses and the new are all within reasonable walking distance, and the walk is getting shorter and shorter.

The New Exhibition Room was on an alley that was no more than a shortcut between Summer and Franklin streets; the first regular theater, called officially the Boston, and more familiarly the Federal Street theater, was two blocks away. The Haymarket opened in 1797 and closed six years later. It stood on Tremont Street opposite the Common, a few blocks away from the first Tremont Theater and near the Boston Museum, which was just around the corner from the Howard Athenaeum. When the Boston Theater on Federal Street closed down in 1852, it was superseded by a mammoth new playhouse of the same name on Washington Street, between Avery and West, within easy walking distance of all these theaters and most of the newer ones, which were constructed

in the last half of the nineteenth century.

There was some theater building when the South End and Back Bay began to develop, but much of it was doomed. On Washington Street in the South End, the Columbia was opened in 1891, a few blocks south of the Globe. Nearby, at the corner of Dover Street, stood the Grand Opera House, which housed melodramas and, at one point, Yiddish-language plays; both are long since gone. So is the Castle Square, a landmark at Tremont and Chandler streets from 1894 till 1932. The National—second theater of that name—opened in 1911; used primarily for variety shows, it is still standing on Tremont Street at Berkeley, and has been marked for renovation. Alongside, the new Boston Arts Center has three dingy rooms used from time to time by the smaller acting companies.

The Back Bay was designed primarily as a residential area and has kept that character, more or less, though many of its fine houses have been taken over in the last fifty years by schools or colleges. But several theaters were built there, and Symphony Hall still stands proudly on Huntington at Massachusetts Avenue, where it has served the community and the world of music since 1901.

A playhouse called at first Chickering Hall, later the St. James Theater, stood on Huntington Avenue a block downtown from Symphony. Thirteen years later, in 1914, some good Bostonians built the Toy Theater (second of that name) on Dartmouth Street, opposite the side entrance of the Copley Plaza. The Toy became the Copley, then the Capri, a movie house; it has long since been razed to make way for the Massachusetts Turnpike Extension. The Boston Opera House, opened in 1909 on Huntington Avenue near the Museum of Fine Arts, was designed for operatic performances, but served many stars and great plays, including the greatest, as the largest of Boston's playhouses; it was bulldozed in 1958.

Only one of the theaters built in the Back Bay is still operating. The original Repertory Theater of Boston, erected in 1925 to house what was meant to be a great resident acting company, closed five years later—a victim, like most theaters

of the kind, of the talkies. But it was restored in 1958 as the Boston University Theatre.

We had a theater-building boom at the beginning of the twentieth century; in twenty-five years, eight new playhouses were constructed in Boston. Except for the Boston Opera House and the original Repertory Theater, all were within easy walking distance of Old Board Alley.

The Colonial opened December 20, 1900, at 106 Boylston Street, the Majestic three years later, around the corner on Tremont Street, near the Shubert and almost opposite the Wilbur. On Stuart Street the Plymouth was erected in 1911.

The Shubert opened on January 24, 1910, with E. H. Sothern and Julia Marlowe in "The Taming of the Shrew," one of four plays in repertory. The new Plymouth brought in the Abbey Theater Company of Dublin at the start of their first American tour a year later. A new playhouse with an old name, the Globe, had begun presenting plays in 1903, two blocks down Stuart Street to the east of the Plymouth. Just about as far in the other direction, the Cort—later the Selwyn—offered its first shows on January 19, 1914.

Of the earlier playhouses, the handsomest was the Boston Theater on Federal Street; the most spectacular, the second Boston; the most curious and most beloved the Boston Museum; the saddest and ultimately the most sordid, the Howard Athenaeum, which passed from grandeur to grossness in the time of its life.

Charles Bulfinch was at the peak of his career

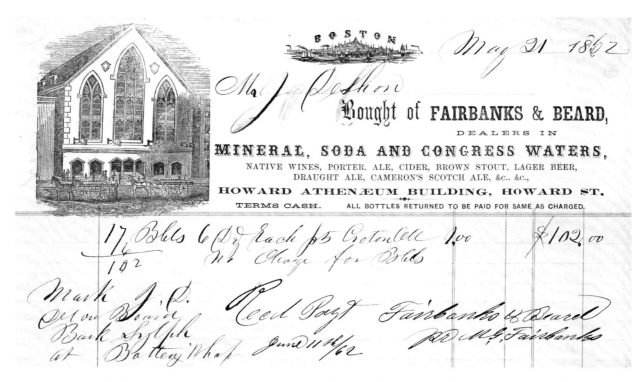

*For many years, the Howard Athenaeum was partly supported by a bottling works in the basement, as this bill indicates. Business was brisk below the stage as well as on it, in 1862.*

Hollis Street Theatre
Boston, Mass.

*The Hollis Street Theater, 1885-1935, one of Boston's most fashionable playhouses, was located on Hollis Street, opposite the present stage entrance of the Metropolitan Theater (Music Hall). The theater was razed in 1935; Hollis Street has since been eliminated.*

when he designed the theater on Federal Street. He had not yet planned the new State House which still graces Beacon Hill, but he had created some lovely houses in the newly developing West End and by his skill and imagination was, as Walter Muir Whitehill put it, "transforming an eighteenth century town into a nineteenth century city."

William W. Clapp, Jr., described Bulfinch's playhouse as "lofty and spacious, substantially built of brick with stone facias, imposts, etc. . . . one hundred and forty feet long, sixty-one feet wide, and forty feet high. . . . In the front there was a projecting arcade, which enabled carriages to land company under cover. The interior of the building was tastefully decorated. The stage opening was thirty-one feet wide, ornamented on each side by two columns, and between them a stage door and projecting iron balcony. Over the columns a cornice and a balustrade were carried across the opening; above was painted a flow of crimson drapery and the arms of the United States and of the State of Massachusetts, blended with emblems tragic and comic. A ribbon depending from the arms bore the motto, 'All the world's a stage.'"

The Haymarket Theater, erected by Bostonians who were unhappy about the way the Federal Street was being run, was described as "an immense wooden pile, overtopping every building in the vicinity"; it had "three tiers of boxes, together with pit and gallery."

The Haymarket was taken down in 1803. Twenty-four years later, the new Tremont became the fashionable showplace of the city, so successful that the "old theater," the Boston, closed two years later and was only open intermittently from then until it was demolished in 1852.

The Boston *Traveler* described the Tremont as "a new and brilliant Temple of the Muses" and avowed that "when it was lighted up on Wednesday evening for the first time . . . the effect was brilliant beyond description." The theater had "a heavy granite front," described as "the admiration of the people," and a handsome interior, with boxes whose fronts were painted blue, and a pit (our present orchestra section) in which "every

seat is cushioned and every other seat is furnished with a back." In that great time, every other Bostonian had a strong and rigid spinal column.

The first Boston Museum and Gallery of Fine Arts opened its doors on June 14, 1841, at the corner of Bromfield Street. A three-story building, it had on the street level "the collection of natural curiosities . . . that formerly belonged to the New England Museum"; these included stuffed animals and birds. On the floor above was "a spacious music saloon." It was in the music saloon that Moses Kimball, the proprietor, presented musical attractions

*The stage of B. F. Keith's Theater on Washington Street between Avery and West. This was one of the first and most famous of all vaudeville theaters, playing two shows a day with all seats reserved. Opened in 1894, it was replaced in 1928 by the new B. F. Keith Memorial Theater (now the Sack Savoy) next door, but was used as a playhouse (Lyric, Apollo) and movie theater (Normandie and Laff Movie) before being razed in 1952.*

and, beginning in 1843, dramatic productions or plays, which became so popular that he built a second Boston Museum with a larger auditorium three blocks north on Tremont Street. The present office building at 18 Tremont Street, next to King's Chapel Burying Ground, stands on the site where his institution flourished until 1893 and existed until 1903; it is appropriately named the Kimball Building.

On December 4, 1846, two days after this new museum-cum-playhouse was opened, the *Daily Transcript* described it as "costly and magnificent" and explained that it was constructed in much the same manner as the earlier building, with "fifty-eight capacious cabinets of curiosities" on the first floor for the edification of museum-goers and up-stairs a handsome theater seating fifteen hundred. "The whole appearance of the house is light and elegant. . . . The stage is fifty feet deep and ninety feet wide, with a proscenium opening thirty feet in width. . . . The audience portion of the house is lighted by three chandeliers and seven candelabras and the gallery is sustained by ten iron columns." Furthermore, reported the *Transcript,* "the scenery is all new, and . . . unequalled for brilliancy and effect . . ." and "the scenes run in iron grooves" so "the audience will no longer be vexed by the creaking, sticking and nonappearance of the wings."

Two blocks away, on Howard Street, the Howard Athenaeum began in a building that had been erected as a temple by the Millerites, who were spending their last days awaiting the end of the world. When the world, for better or worse, just kept rollin' along, a commercial manager rebuilt it in 1845 as a playhouse which burned down only a few months later. Bostonians chose Isaiah Rogers, who had designed the Tremont, as architect of the new playhouse on the same site; a big building in a semi-Gothic style, with a facade of Quincy granite and room enough in its orchestra, boxes, and two balconies for more than two thousand opera buffs, play lovers, and in the final days, Peeping Toms.

In 1854, a new Boston theater was opened on the west side of Washington Street, between Avery West, where theaters had already existed and where several others, some famous, were yet to be constructed. This "Second Boston" was the largest and most luxurious playhouse of its day, and until the Metropolitan moviehouse was built on Tremont Street in 1925, the biggest of all Boston theaters. "Designed," says Douglas Shand Tucci, "by Edward and James Cabot and Jonathan Preston from plans by an otherwise anonymous Henri Noury, its vast domed auditorium seated 3,000. . . ." Dion Boucicault asserted that "it was beyond question the finest theatre in the world."

In 1908, Eugene Tompkins, who had managed the Boston for many years of its glory, was able to write that "even today no theater in the world has been able to surpass it in all important partic-ulars. In beauty of line, in acoustical properties, in ventilation, in ease and economy of heating, in generosity of entrances and lobbies, in comfort and celerity of exit, in size and capability of stage, it has been a model for all the large theaters in this country." The auditorium was "ninety feet in diam-eter and almost circular in shape. . . . The height of the great dome over the auditorium, with its huge chandelier, fifty-four feet . . . the prosce-nium opening forty-eight feet in width by forty-one in height, and the iron fire doors leading from the stage big enough to permit the passage of tally-ho coaches, fire engines or the bulkiest properties that may be needed."

The greatest actors and actresses of the world played the Boston, and, until the Boston Opera House was opened on Huntington Avenue in 1909, the most celebrated opera singers, too, including those of the Metropolitan Opera Company.

There were three theaters in Boston called the Globe, all on Washington Street, all celebrated in their day as showcases for great stars, all within a block or two of one another, making it difficult for puzzled historians to tell one from another. The first, diagonally across Washington Street from the Boston, near the corner of Essex, was christened Selwyn's when it was built in 1867, and that makes for further possible confusion, the more so because in the 1920s a new theater in

*Interior of the Colonial Theater, one of several Boston playhouses designed by C. H. Blackall, showing stage, boxes, and some of the rich decor, which has been preserved intact since 1900.*

Park Square was called (among other names) the Selwyn.

This original Selwyn's became the Globe in 1870, and was burned down three years later in a period when theater fires were common in the United States. The second stood a block farther down Washington Street, on the east side; Sarah Bernhardt played there in 1880. The third Globe was at the corner of Kneeland Street in the present Combat Zone. Opened in 1903, it became in the thirties a burlesque house, ranking in notoriety with the Old Howard; a movie house now, called the Center, it still stands.

The first Tremont, faltering in popularity, closed in 1843, giving way to Tremont Temple. The second was built near the site of the old Haymarket. Home of great plays and players, showcase in the 1920s of such George M. Cohan musical comedies as "Little Nelly Kelly" and "The O'Brien Girl," designed by J. B. McElfatrick, it opened in 1889 on Tremont at Avery Street. Like the Globe, it was fashionable at the end of the nineteenth and the beginning of the twentieth centuries. In 1915, it was used as a movie house to display "The Birth of a Nation," which shook Boston up. In 1948,

its stage was stripped away and it became, and still is, a film theater, now named the Astor.

Another famous playhouse, the Park, was opened on Washington Street a block south of the Boston in 1879. Still standing near the corner of Boylston Street, the Park has had various twentieth-century incarnations. During the early thirties it was Minsky's Park Burlesque where Gypsy Rose Lee took 'em off. Opened on April 14, 1879, with Lotta Crabtree in "La Cigale," it later became little Lotta's own theater, which she watched over during the last years of her life from the Hotel Brewster, where she made her home: it was a house of stars then.

The Columbia, which looked like a Moorish temple on the outside, erected on Washington Street, at the corner of what is now Herald Street, began as a house of grand drama. It had a stock company at one time; later it became a moviehouse. In 1938, the good old Watch and Ward Society found it playing burlesque and warned the manager, who said, Yes, gentlemen, I'll behave. In the meantime, on Hollis Street, which ran between Washington and Tremont, the Hollis Street Theater had opened in 1885 and for fifty years played to fashionable audiences. In 1935, it was razed.

Back on Washington Street, a whole cluster of theaters large and small had opened in the block where the second Boston stood. The most famous of these was B. F. Keith's, which was opened in 1894 to house in elegance Big-Time vaudeville, the kind of variety show that was presented twice a day, with reserved seats and no competing attractions. The B. F. Keith Memorial Theater was erected alongside the vaudeville house on the site of the Boston Theater in 1928; it still stands in a somewhat truncated form as the Sack Savoy movie theater.

As early as 1836, there was a theater called the Lion in this same Washington Street block. In 1839 this became the Melodeon, later the Melodeon Varieties, then, in 1859, the New Melodeon, presenting under these various names such attractions as the Handel and Haydn Society, a concert by Jenny Lind, and various other shows, legitimate

and otherwise. In 1878, the name was changed to Gaiety. Three years later it was remodeled with the auditorium moved to the second floor. On December 18, 1882, the name was again changed; now this upstairs theater, suitable for plays, and for musicals and even opera, was identified as the Bijou.

In 1883, a showman from Hillsborough, N. H., Benjamin Franklin Keith, opened a dime museum on the ground floor of this fecund building, and when that prospered took over the Bijou to operate as a playhouse and, much later, as the Bijou Dream, a film theater. In his museum, which he enlarged and amplified, he began to put on continuous variety shows, designed to please a family trade. It was the success of this variety theater, which operated part of the time in the upstairs Bijou, that led B. F. Keith to open large theaters in other cities, like Providence, devoted to what he was the first to call "vaudeville." It was the popularity and prosperity of the burgeoning chain, the "Keith Circuit," that encouraged him to build and open on March 24, 1894, in the space underneath the Bijou and directly next door to the Boston Theater, his B. F. Keith's Theater.

It was in his honor that subsequent owners of B. F. Keith's, the Bijou, and the Boston decided to raze the Boston and to build on the site the Keith Memorial Theater, which opened in splendor on Monday evening, October 29, 1928. Described as "a dazzling architectural dream in ivory and gold, with sixteen great marble columns," it had walnut paneling and impressive oil paintings on its walls, and it was meant to continue in glory the Keith tradition of Big-Time Vaudeville. Unfortunately, the Big Time was already dying, and the Small Time, too.

When the Memorial opened, the B. F. Keith Theater was taken over by the Shuberts of New York and operated by them for four years as the Apollo and then as the Lyric, presenting Broadway plays and musicals. Later, it became a moviehouse called the Normandie, then the Laff Movie; it was razed in the fifties. Earlier, in 1913, Keith had bought the old Boston, had rented it as a legitimate theater to New York interests, and had then opened it as the Keith Boston to vaudeville and films. When they tore it down in 1925, his successors built another Keith Boston across Washington Street at the corner of Essex; this three-thousand-seat house became the Cyclorama, then the Essex.

Long before Keith came to Boston, the Boston Music Hall was operating a few blocks away. Although it presented plays for only a brief period in 1902, when the Castle Square stock company moved in while their playhouse was being renovated, it made history as a concert hall where the Boston Symphony Orchestra played before the opening of Symphony Hall, and it has recently been reclaimed as a temporary home by the Opera Company of Boston. This Music Hall (not to be confused with the present Music Hall on Tremont Street opposite the Shubert) was built with an entrance on Hamilton Place, just off Tremont Street, near Winter. It was remodeled twice and—of course—had its name changed, first to the Empire, then to the Orpheum, and later, in 1915, to Loew's Orpheum, when it began to be used as a movie and vaudeville theater. In 1905, as the Empire, it got a new, second entrance on Washington Street: a long marble hall, with mirrors and a rather considerable flight of stairs.

In "The Boston Rialto: Playhouses, Concert Halls, and Movie Palaces," Douglass Tucci points out that despite the additions and alterations, the original theater has survived to this day. "Boston's first concert hall," he writes, "became (in 1915), her first movie palace . . . with a sweeping, pastel Adamesque interior, complete with a crystal proscenium arch lit by hundreds of electric lights," designed by Thomas Lamb when he did it over for Marcus Loew. It is less elegant now, but still useful for Sarah Caldwell and her Opera Company of Boston, who use it while waiting for the day when they can construct a new opera house.

The Castle Square Theater, which was small compared to such great caverns as the Boston, yet elegant in the rococo style, opened in 1894 on Tremont Street at Chandler, in the South End.

Its stock company, operated between 1908 and 1916 by John Craig and Mary Young, was popular during that period, but it succumbed in 1929 to the movie competition and was razed in 1932.

The twentieth-century building boom that gave us our present playhouses began with the opening in 1900 of the Colonial. Designed by Clarence H. Blackall, an extraordinary architect who drew the plans for other notable theaters, it is built within the confines of an office building. Its exterior is undistinguished, but within all is good taste and elegance now, as it was in the beginning. Seating seventeen hundred in an auditorium with commodious boxes and two big balconies, it is, to quote Mr. Tucci, "as sumptuous and elegant as any of the productions its proscenium has disclosed. Its lavish carved detail is the work of John Evans Company. . . . The extensive sequence of murals Blackall and Pennell collaborated on are of their type and period unique in Boston." The great frieze in the dome of the auditorium (the three standing male figures were designed to portray Tradition, Truth, and Inspiration between pairs of figures representing the dances) was painted by Herman Schladermunt. Schladermunt and his assistants also executed the four seated female figures in the adjoining circles, which are entitled "Epic Poetry," "History," "Tragedy," and "Comic or Pastoral Verse."

The Colonial is not only handsome, it is also intimate: its auditorium, designed in a wide fan shape, seems to bring actors close to the audience, and it is admirably well-equipped to present anything from domestic comedy to grand opera. The smaller Wilbur, dating from 1914, stands alone, simple and proud, on Tremont Street at the corner of Stuart, the only distinguished structure in that area. Also designed by Blackall, it is three stories high, in colonial brick, its portals modeled after those of the Thomas Bailey Aldrich house on Beacon Hill, with a modest balcony directly overhead. The auditorium is uncluttered, in an almost severe modern style. There are lobbies on the orchestra and balcony floors and a lounge in the basement. The stage is broad and reasonably deep, admirable

for comedies like "Mary, Mary" or dramas like "Our Town," both of which were first tested there, or for such newer productions as "Hair," "Godspell," or "Equus," all of which have played the Wilbur with notable success.

The Shubert, across the street, is utilitarian rather than elegant—suitable for all kinds of shows, reasonably comfortable, but architecturally undistinguished. Not so the Majestic, another in the Tremont Street cluster. Like the Plymouth, it was converted to movies in 1957, but it is still impressive in the fashion of the nineteenth century. Designed by John Galen Howard, opened in 1903 with a fashionable gala, it is richly scarlet and gold with lovely arches over rows of boxes that suggest Viennese splendor. Like the Colonial, it was cunningly conceived to provide a feeling of intimacy. Until it was sold to the Sack movie chain and rechristened the Saxon, it served as an elegant home for drama and musical shows, and might well be reclaimed for glory by angels with pockets full of money, a flair for opulence, and a good commercial connection to the United Booking Office of New York.

The first of two Boston playhouses to be called the Toy Theater opened on Lime Street at the foot of Beacon Hill in 1911. Like the New Exhibition Room of 1792, our first playhouse, and The Next Move at 955 Boylston Street, our latest (opened in 1977), it was made from a stable; it seated no more than a hundred friends.

The second Toy Theater, erected in 1914, was five times as large and reasonably opulent. On Dartmouth Street, opposite the Copley Plaza, it had a handsome bow front that led to the nickname "Round House," and inside a pair of staircases, handsome parentheses, donated by Isabella Gardner—"Mrs. Jack"—of Beacon Street and the Fenway. A year later, the Toy became the Copley, which in 1922 was pulled back, split in two, extended and expanded, and, without its bow front, turned around to face Stuart Street in a rather extraordinary engineering feat that required the use of horse-drawn drays. In 1957 when, like the Keith Memorial, the Plymouth, and the Majestic, it

Majestic Theater on Tremont Street near Boylston.
Opened 1903, became Saxon Movie Theater in '58.

was taken over by the Sack movie theater chain
it was further altered to allow for entrance on
Huntington Avenue, the third side of the triangular
plot on which it had been constructed. When
progress, or whatever, decided that the Massachusetts Turnpike must be extended into Boston,
it and the other buildings of that triangle were
bulldozed; nothing remains but a plot of grass.

Symphony Hall was built in 1901, designed in
classical beauty by McKim, Mead and White,
endowed with perfect acoustics by Wallace Sabine
of Harvard, an original genius, and provided with
a massive open stage and twenty-nine hundred
seats on the floor and two balconies. Although it
was created for the Boston Symphony Orchestra,
it has housed theatrical entertainments and from
time to time plays: the First Drama Quartet, that
brilliant team of Shavians consisting of Agnes
Moorhead, Charles Laughton, Cedric Hardwicke,
Charles Boyer, read Shaw's "Don Juan in Hell"
there in 1951, and on February 5, 1971, for one
night only, Judith Anderson tried and, sadly, failed
as Hamlet on its great stage.

Across from Symphony Hall, sleek and trim,
with nine hundred seats in an intimate auditorium,
stands the original Repertory Theater of Boston,
opened in 1925 under the management of Henry
Jewett. Closed five years later, when the talkies
began to obliterate the stock and repertory companies, it has since been used for movies and for
an occasional touring play like "Life with Father";
in the thirties, it served as the Boston home of the
Federal Theater Project. In 1958, Boston University
bought and has since restored it to beauty and use-
fulness as the Boston University Theatre.

Farther out on Huntington Avenue, the Boston
Opera House was opened in 1909. A vast brick
pile with marble halls and corridors, it seated
twenty-nine hundred patrons in considerable comfort and unchallenged gilt-and-gold splendor, with
a ring of properly private boxes facing a stage
that was seventy-five feet deep. The merchant
Eben Jordan made the Opera House possible in
order to house visiting opera companies and, in its
time, our own Boston Opera Company. But opera
companies dwindled down to a precious few, and
during most of its life the building was owned and
operated by the Shuberts of New York, who presented there musical comedies, occasional plays
like "The Barretts of Wimpole Street" with
Katharine Cornell, and operettas, until one day
in 1956 when the city building department suggested that it needed substantial repairs. There was

some question as to whether it was actually safe, whether its foundations in the waters of the Back Bay could, or should, be shored up. But J. J. Shubert, who had kept it open for years despite a grave paucity of bookings, decided abruptly and heatedly to sell it, and there was nobody to shout him down. It was razed to make way for a Northeastern University dormitory.

In the years since then, the Metropolitan Opera Company has appeared at the Metropolitan Theater, the huge moviehouse on Tremont Street that is now known as the Music Hall (second of that name) and, more recently, at the Hynes Memorial Auditorium on Boylston Street. Sarah Caldwell's Opera Company of Boston presented its great operatic shows in various locations, including a tent at the Massachusetts Institute of Technology and a bleak gymnasium at Tufts University, before settling in the Orpheum Theater.

As the Metropolitan, the present Music Hall was opened with a Hollywoodish gala in 1925 as a movie theater, one of the first great cinematic shrines which the industry called "de luxe picture palaces" and which, because of their beauty, their comfort, and the cheapness of their best shows, did much to put out of business all the stock companies and many of the competing legitimate theaters. Designed by Blackall, the Metropolitan was larger than the great Boston Theater on Washington Street, handsomer than the Colonial, and, with 4,210 seats, more capacious than any playhouse in Boston's history.

In the 1920s and for many subsequent years, Hollywood was apt to confuse gaudiness with beauty; Blackall was not. The theater he planned, with its entrance on Tremont Street, was and still is, though faded now, a magnificent structure, with a large mezzanine and big balconies hovering over a

*The Shubert Theater which opened in 1910 is still the home of hits, at 265 Tremont Street.*

huge, comfortable auditorium and a wide, if un-fortunately shallow, stage. The entrance lobby is in marble, with a grand marble staircase and mirrored doors in the gallery above. Like the Keith Memorial, it had handsome paintings on its walls and rich fixtures, even gold-plated doorknobs, on the lobby gallery, until the vandalism of World War II forced the owners to put all valuables away forever and to shrug off as best they could the regular slashing of seats and even the theft of bathroom fixtures by juveniles equipped with knives, wrenches, and a cynical disregard for property rights.

With a feature film, a stage show, and a seventy-piece orchestra at a top ticket price of seventy cents, the Metropolitan flourished until the Department of Justice forced the Paramount Pictures Corporation to divest itself of its theaters. The New England Medical Center, expanding its great teaching-hospital complex from a base on Harrison Avenue (and, at one time, with an eye on Park Square), bought it and the adjacent Wilbur Theater, too. As the Music Hall, it played some of the big ballet companies, but the shallowness of its stage made it unsuitable for the greatest of the dance companies and for the Metropolitan Opera Company. In 1977, with a new and well-planned campaign under way to reconstruct the stage and restore the theater to its original beauty (probably with its original name), a Broadway musical was booked into the Music Hall for the first time. The Houston Grand Opera Company, forced with the choice between charging $19.00 a ticket in the Colonial, which seats seventeen hundred, and the possibility of paying off at $12.50 in the Music Hall, chose the bigger theater in an experimental move.

The Charles Playhouse and the other small theaters that sprang up in the city as the regional theater movement began to develop in the fifties and the sixties are all makeshifts. On Warrenton Street behind the Shubert, the Charles occupies a former nightclub called the Lido Venice which had been made from an old church designed by Asher Benjamim. The first playhouse in the city to abandon the old proscenium stage, it has five

hundred rigidly upright chairs on three sides of a rectangular thrust stage.

The Boston Arts Center, at 551 Tremont Street, is a conglomerate of old brick buildings in which three small rooms have been used by theater companies. Alongside is the vast old pile of the National Theater, which was opened in 1911 as the Waldorf; it has shown vaudeville and movies sporadically and is marked for possible restoration by the Boston Redevelopment Authority. In all fairness, it needs to be pointed out that the grimly unattractive theaters of this Arts Center have served to house companies that were otherwise without a home. But none have stayed long, preferring to move into one or another of the church halls that have been made available to them at a fee.

*Wilbur Theater, on Tremont Street, opened in 1914— one of America's handsomest playhouses.*

The Boston Repertory Theater troupe—about which more later—used the Arts Center, then rented space in a church hall, and finally in 1976, got the money to convert a recording studio at One Boylston Place into a tiny playhouse that seats 232 people in reasonable comfort. The Next Move Company, a comparable troupe of young players, shifted their scenery to various addresses before finding at 955 Boylston Street in the Back Bay a stable that had been used by the mounted police. Having carefully swept it clean, they found two hundred chairs, built an acting space, and moved in. Such other local troupes as the Theater Company of Boston have similarly created their own acting spaces, only to lose them to landlords with other plans. The T.C.B., for example, began in 1963 with a ninety-place playhouse in the Hotel Bostonian, on Boylston Street near Massachusetts Avenue; they lost that to a school. They built another, larger space in an old dining room of the Hotel Touraine, at Tremont and Boylston, and the hotel closed down. Then they made over the Fenway movie theater on Massachusetts Avenue, only to lose that, too, to a school that bought the building for a legitimate expansion.

The only new structures built as theaters in the Greater Boston area since the Repertory Theater of Boston was erected in 1925 are owned and operated by universities. Fortunately, they are made available for professional attractions open to the public. On Brattle Street in Cambridge, just off Harvard Square, Harvard opened the seven-hundred-seat Loeb Drama Center in 1959. Designed by Hugh Stubbins, this is a modern brick structure with the most flexible stage in New England, suitable for any kind of production in any form, from arena to proscenium at the touch of a button or the whim of a director. Each year, in addition to productions of the Harvard Dramatic Club, its managers present touring productions, and, in July and August, offer plays by the Harvard Summer Repertory Theater. In Waltham, Max Abramowitz is the architect of the circular brick Spingold Theater, which sits proudly on a hill above the Music Center and below the Rose Art Museum of

*Playbill for "The Unforeseen" by Robert Marshall, the final attraction of the Boston Museum, week of May 11, 1903. Note that the actors were under the management of Charles Frohman of New York; the famous stock company had closed ten years earlier.*

Brandeis University. It has three playhouses, the largest with seven hundred seats; all are simple, comfortable, and useful for student productions and for those outside attractions that can be displayed there in a period when costs usually require greater seating capacity. The fact that its principal theater is shaped like a pie wedge gives the interior an odd piquancy which directors may or may not appreciate when they marshal their actors in the hope of making all of them visible at all times.

# CHAPTER III

## THE PLAYERS ARE WELL BESTOWED: THE BRITISH...

In Boston, the first actors were British soldiers, performing in Faneuil Hall in 1775 and putting on such plays as pleased them, including General John Burgoyne's apparently noxious farce, "The Blockade of Boston," and their ladies, recruited from the Tories of Boston. When the time came for "moral lectures" more than a century later, there were no actors in red coats and ladies of the town were not present, but again the casts were English, and it is a fact of Boston's theatrical history that England has supplied us with a long line of good and great actors right down to the present; and except in rare cases, as in 1825 when our play-goers chased the tragedian Edmund Kean out of town, running for his life, and 1971, when Judith Anderson failed to please in "Hamlet," they have been hospitably received.

Nobody is sure where the first producer engaged his performers for the moral lectures at the New Exhibition Room in 1792, but it seems likely they were stragglers from the old American Company of Lewis and William Hallam, which had played in New York and other cities on the coast since before the Revolution. But when the lights went on in the lovely new theater in Federal Street, the manager, Charles Stuart Powell, had a company he had recruited the year before in London; there were no Americans, though there would be many later on before the old theater was finally closed.

When the new Boston Theater was erected on Washington Street in 1854, the new manager followed the precedent established by his predecessor at Federal Street. He visited London to recruit his cast, and hired one entire family of English players. Although he admitted in a letter written to his assistant back home that he took the lot in order to get two pretty teenage daughters, he testified that Mom and Dad were competent, too, and their four small children would be able to take such roles as those of the boy princes in "King Richard III." When his theater opened on September 21, 1804, manager Joseph Barry had guest stars in for the first performances of Sheridan's "The Rivals"—actors from New York, Philadelphia, Manchester, and Dublin. Members of the Biddles family of London were not in that play or in the farce that followed, but Clara Biddles, one of the two pretty sisters, sat in a stage box with him, and not long after, the records indicate, she became Mrs. Thomas Barry. An astute fellow, Tom Barry, and an honorable one, too: not every show-man who has hired a pretty actress has gone so far as to offer matrimony. Or was it Clara, supported by Mom and Dad, who insisted?

Before Tom Barry's adventure in London, his predecessors at the older Boston Theater, at the short-lived Haymarket, at the Tremont, the Boston Museum, and the Howard Athenaeum had also been importing the great stars of London, and would go on doing so. Their successors still are, though now, of course, the practice is to bring them in with an entire supporting company. In Barry's day the custom was to invite a star to appear as a guest with the local resident players—the "stock," as they were called.

The first of the stars with a great London reputation was brilliant on the stage, and, like quite a few who followed down the years, not very well-behaved outside the theater. George Frederick Cooke was notably unreliable, likely to arrive at the playhouse long after he had been expected; but he could act when he felt like it with stunning

effect, and his "semi-occasional sprees," which killed him at the age of fifty-five, seem not to have prevented him from giving great performances at the Federal Street Theater, where he opened in a municipal buzz of excitement on January 3, 1811. He pleased just about everyone in a repertory of great plays, and like most of the English in the years to follow was himself pleased by the Boston response.

In our own time, the stars of London have often chosen to play only in Boston or New York and perhaps Washington, disdaining other American cities as potentially unsympathetic; several have become so enamored that they have thought about settling down here. John Wood of the Royal Shakespeare Company, ending a tour in "Travesties" before Boston audiences that were alert and responsive, stayed over three days after the play closed to shop in Filene's Basement and to enjoy the city itself, and before he went back to England put an advertisement in the *Globe:* "Thank you, Boston. Love, John Wood."

There is no evidence, so far as I know, that George Frederick Cooke fell in love with the city back in 1811 (though he may, perhaps, have developed a friendly relationship with a number of bartenders), but playgoers loved him, and made him temporarily rich. Between the third and the twenty-fourth of January 1811, acting Monday through Friday (the Puritan Sabbath began Saturday at sundown and until 1871 performances were forbidden on that night), he appeared in eight plays, including his greatest: "King Richard III," "Othello," "The Merchant of Venice," and "King Henry IV, Part One." During that time he earned as his share of the receipts $3,640.68, tax-free.

Eleven months later, he came back again for nineteen additional nights, adding this time from his repertory "King Lear," "Macbeth," and Massinger's "A New Way to Pay Old Debts," a popular favorite in which he seems to have been grand as the overreaching Sir Giles Overreach. This time his wages ran to $3,200, or almost enough to make it worthwhile for a contemporary rock star to leave his pad and tune up his guitar. A few weeks later, having lost the battle of the bottle, Cooke was dead and buried in New York.

Edmund Kean, an ill-starred genius who had behavior problems, too, but who was an even greater actor—very likely the greatest since David Garrick, and the most accomplished of all Englishmen till the rise of Laurence Olivier—made his first Boston appearances at the Old Federal Street Theater nine years after Cook's farewell. Like some of his predecessors (Garrick, for one) and his contemporaries, Edmund Kean was a small man, so diminutive that when he performed in London in "Alexander the Great," a noisy spectator at one performance offered loudly the suggestion that he had better be named "Alexander the Little." To which, according to one story, Kean replied from the stage, "Yes, but great of soul."

There is little reason to believe that Edmund was great of soul, but in the major tragic roles of the English-language repertory he brought audiences at Covent Garden and Drury Lane to their feet

*Edmund Kean, an actor of power and virtuosity. He pleased Bostonians until he became temperamental— then they chased him out of town.*

time and again when he played "King Lear" or "King Richard III." In Boston, making his debut on February 12, 1821, he got no standing ovations in "Lear" and "Hamlet" and J. H. Payne's "Brutus"; Bostonians hadn't got around to that dubious response in those days. But his popularity was enormous during nine nights of performance; so when the audience shouted for him to stay longer, he took it as an invitation for the immediate future, and in so doing made a catastrophic mistake. His friends warned him that Bostonians of that day didn't got to the theater in May, there being no air conditioning and so many things to do outside. But he heeded them not at all, booked himself back to the Boston, and opened here on May 23 in "King Lear." Business was not good. Three nights later, there were only a handful of people on hand to see his "King Richard III" and that annoyed Edmund Kean so much that he refused to go on; he walked out of the theater, and left behind an indignant audience.

Four years later, in 1825, he returned to Boston and they were waiting for him. He had offered apologies, humble and even abject, through the newspapers, and some, at least, of the patrons were ready to forgive and hear him out, but not a great crowd of men and boys who filled the pit and Federal Street outside. They roared him down when he appeared, and when he tried to placate them refused in a great din of protest to listen. When he finally quit the stage, they took over the playhouse in a wild and contemptible riot that destroyed almost everything. Kean himself got out of the neighborhood in disguise and was taken in a private coach over the causeway to Brighton, where he took the stagecoach to New York. He was lucky to get away with his life. We must not believe that all Bostonians of those days were proper.

That incident was unique, of course, and unforgivable. In New York a few years later, on May 10, 1849, a comparable crowd created such a frightful uproar at the appearance of another English star, William Charles Macready, that the militia was called out, and in the melee that followed outside the Astor Place Opera House twenty-two people were shot and killed and thirty-six wounded.

There were no shots fired as Edmund Kean scampered away to Brighton, and there was no disturbance here when Macready appeared in Boston a year after the Kean shambles, making his debut in the first of several successful visits. Like Kean and Cooke and too many of the others, he was an actor of enormous power and excitement in tragedy and sometimes a bad actor offstage.

Bostonians knew what was going on in London in those days. When Macready opened at the old theater in Federal Street on October 30, 1826, in "Virginius," the house was packed with proper and the other kind of Bostonians, Daniel Webster being of course in the first category. Daniel got a hand when he walked in and Macready was saluted with affection and admiration. Tickets for his engagement were sold at auction, which was a custom in the nineteenth century. (When Jenny Lind sang at the Music Hall twenty-five years later, the auctioneers got $645 for one ticket.) In Boston, "the only American city he liked," Macready pleased playgoers in "Virginius" and in the other classics, among them "Macbeth" and "Hamlet," that were part of the repertory of all these great stars. The next year he was back gain, and there were many later visits, one in "Macbeth" at the Howard Athenaeum beginning on October 30, 1848, only a few months before New Yorkers disgraced themselves and damaged for years the good name of the theater and of all actors in the Astor Place riot.

In the meantime, still another great Londoner, Junius Brutus Booth, had come to Boston for the first of many visits in which he would alternately thrill and bewilder our audiences. Junius was also, alas, an alcoholic and in his later years was mentally depressed. When on one occasion he wandered away from the Tremont Theater half-dressed and shoeless and set out to walk to Providence, it was generally blamed on drink, but he was probably out of his mind, suffering from the torments that in our day would have sent him to a psychiatrist at $150 an hour. Junius opened in "King Rich-

ard III" at Federal Street, and was accepted at once as one of the greatest personators of that "bunch-back'd toad." He seems to have acted by flashes of lightning, dropping from grandeur to apathy as the spirit, or spirits, moved him, then surging again in power to lift up the hearts of his audiences.

Junius played in Boston and everywhere across the country, returning each summer to his home near Baltimore to raise vegetables and to cultivate his nine children. The children were his by a good woman whom he had brought from England, leaving behind a wife, one son, and two illegitimate children. He was faithful to his mistress if not to his wife, and eventually, in 1854, managed a divorce from the first Mrs. Booth. In the meantime, three of his children had gone into the theater, as actors. The oldest, Edwin, would become the greatest of all American players, unequalled till the time of John Barrymore. A second son, Junius, Jr., was a good performer who served in Boston for a time as manager of the Tremont Theater. The third was John Wilkes Booth, whose mind was as twisted as his father's and whose impulses were not so good. On April 14, 1865, while Edwin Booth was acting at the Boston Theater in Washington Street, John slipped into a box at Ford's Theater in Washington, shot and killed President Abraham Lincoln, and escaped by jumping onto the stage and riding away on a horse.

The Booths were one of the great American acting dynasties sprung from visiting English stars. The Barrymores were another, descended on one side from a London actor named Herbert Blyth, who called himself Maurice Barrymore when he landed in Boston in 1875; he had seen the name on a paper somewhere in London, liked it, adopted it, and used it when he acted at the Boston Theater in his American debut, playing among other roles the title part in "The Shaughraun" by Dion Boucicault.

Maurice had a spectacular and brilliant career marred by temperamental behavior on and off the stage, but is most famous for his descendants. A year after his American premiere performances in

Boston, he married Georgiana Drew of Philadelphia, an actress of distinction, daughter of Louisa Lane Drew and her husband, John, and sister of stars; Georgiana became the mother of John, Ethel, and Lionel Barrymore.

In George S. Kaufman and Edna Ferber's comedy "The Royal Family," which opened in 1927 and was reproduced successfully in 1976, the Drews and the Barrymores are represented in a fictional story that draws on the facts to create a lot of fun and to suggest something of their loyalties to one another and to the stage. The central character of the play, Mrs. Cavendish, is modelled mostly after old Mrs. John Drew, born Louisa Lane in London, the mother-in-law of Maurice and grandmother of Ethel, John, and Lionel (who called her "Mum-Mum"). The daughter is most like Ethel; and Tony Cavendish, the prankish son, resembles John, who was as erratic and temperamental as any of the stars in any of the dynasties.

There were of course other dynasties, and most of their progeny played Boston. The Kembles, for instance. The two greatest Kembles undoubtedly were John Phillip and his sister Sarah, who, under her married name, Mrs. Siddons, was generally considered the greatest tragedienne of England. John Phillip was an elegant actor, rival in the classic roles of the cruder but more powerful Edmund Kean.

Neither Sarah nor John Philip got to America, but their brother Charles, a star in his own right, and their niece, Fanny Kemble (Charles' daughter), played here with great success, Charles and Fanny came to Boston as co-stars and almost didn't make it because their salaries were so high. The manager of the Tremont Theater was afraid he couldn't pay them and the rest of the actors, not to mention his other costs. But he arranged a deal, and, as one historian wrote, still in a daze twenty years later, "Fanny came among us as an adorable divinity with all the halo of her transAtlantic triumphs. . . ." Like all the stars of that period, the Kembles played repertory, opening April 15, 1833, with "Hamlet," in which Dad was the prince and Fanny, who had served him as Ophelia in London, did not appear.

Edmund Kean as Othello.

They were together, however, in "Romeo and Juliet," sharing the two star roles; there being no psychiatrists in those days, there were no murmurings, only exclamations of enthusiasm.

Fanny was a rare beauty, slender and ladylike. Dad had the bearing of a gentleman and, although he was slightly deaf, great skill in such plays as one by the Reverend H. H. Milmann called "Fazio, or the Italian Wife," and in "The School for Scandal." Father and daughter created, in the words of William W. Clapp, Jr., "an excitement in the dramatic world of Boston and vicinity. Tickets were sold at auction, and crowded houses, composed of the beauty and wealth of the city, assembled to hear Miss Kemble and her father." Later, after she married and then divorced a Philadelphian named Pierce Butler, Fanny gave up the stage and for some time lived in Lenox, Mass., where she received some of our most celebrated citizens and from which she came forth to give readings at Harvard College, where she was introduced by Professor Henry Wadsworth Longfellow, and throughout the country; Fanny's Shakespearean readings became part of the culture of the United States.

In her biography, *"Fanny Kemble, a Passionate Victorian,* Margaret Armstrong wrote: "She would come stepping on the stage, bow with grave dignity right and left, seat herself, spread out her flowing skirts, and open her little book: with the first word, an audience would be hers. For three generations of Americans, Fanny Kemble's was a name to conjure with. . . ." Admirers of her Shakespearean readings included Henry James, Henry Cabot Lodge, Louisa Alcott, and even Emerson. Her performances were "readings" and not performances, "for," to quote Ms. Armstrong again, "the backwash of the Evangelical movement was still dampening the ardor of American theatergoers, and Shakespeare readings were considered an agreeable compromise between dangerous wordly amusements and no amusements at all." This, after all, was the period in which Bostonians were patronizing the Boston Museum in the stated belief

*Mrs. Kendal of London, who co-starred with her husband. They were both much admired in Boston, professionally and personally.*

that it was, after all, a museum and "not really a theater."

After the Kembles, father and daughter, the rowdier English stars gave way to ladies and gentlemen and eventually to knights and ladies, some of them paired as partners, and as husbands and wives, too. Bostonians rejoiced with the Kendals, W. H. and his wife; with the great Henry Irving and Ellen Terry; and with Johnston Forbes-Robertson and Gertrude Elliott; with Mr. and Mrs. Herbert Beerbohm-Tree, and many others.

Henry Irving and Ellen Terry co-starred first at the Boston Theater on Washington Street in 1883 and 1884 with his London Lyceum Theater Com-

pany in a repertory of classic plays, among them "The Merchant of Venice," in which he was Shylock and she Portia; then at the Tremont in 1893 and 1894. The Irving favorites included an old melodrama called "The Bells," which Eugene O'Neill mentions in "A Long Day's Journey into Night" as the play that old James Tyrone, Sr. played for twenty years, that made him rich and that he hated. Irving and Terry were here again at the Tremont, opening October 7, 1895, in a "legendary play" called "King Arthur," he as the king, Ellen as Guinevere—roles to be tested sixty-five years later in Boston by two other English stars, Richard Burton and Julie Andrews, in another version of the same story, "Camelot," at the Shubert Theater.

Henry Irving was knighted by Queen Victoria in 1895. After Irving and Terry, London sent the new ranking star, Johnston Forbes-Robertson, with *his* leading lady, Gertrude Elliott, an American girl who was—in whatever private life he had—his wife. At the Hollis Street Theater on January 14, 1907, they presented George Bernard Shaw's "Caesar and Cleopatra" for pleased Bostonians, who knew by his bearing that he would be the next English actor to become a knight, Sir Johnston. His knighthood came only at the end of his career, during the final week of his farewell performances in London in 1913.

Since then, we have seen and admired most of the knights created by kings and queens, and some of these have been in the true royalty of the English stage, and in style and skill have ranked with their more flamboyant and less mannerly predecessors of the nineteenth century. John Gielgud, who would become Sir John in 1953, gave his first and grandest performance here on February 6, 1936, at the Shubert Theater in "Hamlet," the greatest "Hamlet" this generation of Bostonians had seen except, perhaps, John Barrymore's. I say "perhaps" because Barrymore, who played in the role in New York for 101 performances and for one week in 1923 at the Boston Opera House, was erratic and irresponsible and acted well only when

he happened to feel like it.

A year before Gielgud, another Englishman, Leslie Howard, had tried the taxing role and had not done well, either in a Boston tryout at the Opera House or in a subsequent engagement in New York during which he and Gielgud played the role in opposition. Howard had been a movie matinee idol and, as he proved here and in New York in 1934 in "The Petrified Forest," with considerable support from a then-unknown American named Humphrey Bogart, a fine actor of modern plays. He was an intelligent and appealing Hamlet, but in the doublet and hose of the Elizabethans seemed a little frail, and in a blond wig he looked, as one jealous star (Philip Merivale) also English, said, "a little like Peter Pan."

In New York, Gielgud roused most of the critics to a tumult of enthusiasm. Howard, to the great indignation of his movie fans, did not. Howard went on the road. Gielgud stayed, then made for Boston, to prove himself again. Very young, delicately handsome and elegant in Hamlet's black weeds, he spoke the speeches in the most richly musical voice the modern stage had yet heard, and played with passion that blazed out in the great scenes and the rich soliloquies; and unlike Barrymore, he did it night after night. In his own words, he could only give his best performances about three times a week—"eight is really too many"—but nobody caught him napping or at least not trying during the other five.

Sir John has played Boston many times since then, electing to try some of his new productions, like "The Lady's Not for Burning," at the Shubert prior to Broadway. In Christopher Fry's poetic fantasy, the audience at the Shubert on the opening night, October 23, 1950, was disturbed by the acoustics and by some of the accents of the London cast who, except for Gielgud, had not learned to speak up to fill the big playhouse; but they were stirred by the star and, most of them, by a young actor in the small role of Richard: Richard Burton, some of them decided, had a personality and a style of his own. Later, as Gielgud came back in

# BOSTON MUSEUM

ESTABLISHED 1841

30th WEEK OF THE

Mr. R. M. FIELD — MANAGER

40th REGULAR SEASON.

---

"A STOCK COMPANY THAT HAS BEEN THE DELIGHT OF GENERATIONS OF BOSTONIANS."—*Transcript.*

"Nothing useless is, or low;
Each thing in its place is best;

And what seems but idle show,
Strengthens and supports the rest."—*Longfellow.*

---

 **GRAND SUCCESS**

and **Fourth Week** of the engagement of the Distinguished Dramatist and Actor, MR.

## DION BOUCICAULT

AND FOR

ONE WEEK ONLY, "THE COLLEEN BAWN."

Monday, March 21, 1881, and

Every Evening at 7 3-4; also on Wednesday and Saturday Afternoons at 2,

MR. BOUCICAULT'S GREAT PLAY.

## The Colleen Bawn

FOR ITS FIRST TIME HERE IN MANY YEARS.

MR. DION BOUCICAULT as

MYLES-NA-COPPALEEN (Myles of the Ponies)

SUPPORTED BY THE FOLLOWING BOSTON MUSEUM CAST:

| | |
|---|---|
| Hardress Cregan, son of Mrs. Cregan | Mr. J. S. Haworth |
| Kyrle Daly, a college friend to Hardress | Mr. B. R. Graham |
| Father Tom, Parish Priest of Garryowen | Mr. Alfred Hudson |
| Mr. Corrigan, a half-Sir | Mr. J. Burrows |
| Danny Mann, the hunchback servant | Mr. Wm. Seymour |
| Mr. O'Moore, a magistrate | Mr. J. B. Mason |
| Hyland Creagh | Mr. Maurice Strafford |
| Corporal | Mr. J. S. Maffitt, Jr. |
| Servant | Mr. Chas. E. Hogle |
| Anne Chute, the Colleen Ruadh | Miss Annie Clarke |
| Eily O'Connor, the Colleen Bawn | Miss Sadie Martinot |
| Sheelah | Mrs. J. R. Vincent |
| Mrs. Cregan | Miss Mary Shaw |
| Ducie Blennerhasset | Miss Rose Temple |
| Kathleen Creagh | Miss Kate Miriam |

Soldiers, Guests, Servants, etc.

NEW AND ELEGANT SCENERY, NOVEL MECHANICAL EFFECTS, RICH APPOINTMENTS, ORIGINAL MUSIC, etc.

### SYNOPSIS OF SCENERY AND INCIDENTS:

**ACT FIRST.**

The Lakes of Killarney by Moonlight. The Irish Leander; the Proposal; the Light on Mucross Head; thrice it goes in and thrice it goes out; the Signal; the Assignation with the Colleen Bawn. Scene 2.—The Gap of Dunaloe. Myles of the Ponies; the Bride; Myles engaged as a Spy. Scene 3.—The Cottage of the Colleen Bawn. The Jug of Punch; the Irish Cottage Fireside; The Crooskeen Lawn; the Marriage Lines; The Oath.

**ACT SECOND.**

Scene 1.—The Gap. The Proposal to Danny Mann; "Give me your glove and I'll clear the Colleen from your path;" the Token. Scene 2.—Torc Cregan House. The Resolve; the Glove; the Death Warrant. Scene 3.—Torc

Lake and M'Gillicuddy's Reeks. "The Pretty Girl Milking her Cow;" Eily O'Connor; Anne Chute; The Two Brides Face to Face; the Colleen Ruadh and the Colleen Bawn; the Irish Lady and the Irish Peasant Girl. Scene 4.—The Thunder-Storm; the Shelter; Eily's Letter of adieu. Scene 5. Myles' Watch-House. The Rope and the Entry to O'Donahoe's Stables. Scene 6.—The Water Cave. The Flying Bridge. A puzzle for the Gaugers. The Demand and The Murder.

**ACT THIRD.**

Sheelah's Hut. The Dying Boy; the Confession; Corrigan in a Turf Hole; the Spy obtains evidence. Scene 2.—The Parlor in Castle Chute. The Two Friends; the Mistake. Scene 3.—Myles' Cottage. The Mysterious Inhabitant; Myles in a corner. Scene 4.—The Outskirts of Castle Chute. Corrigan in his glory; the Sentinels surrounding the house. Scene 5.—The Ball-Room in Castle Chute on the banks of the Shannon. A Card; the first mutterings of the storm; the Two Women in defence of the Criminal; the Attack and the Tumult; the Resistance; the Arrest; the Investigation; the Dying Man's Confession; the Glove; Myles' Witness. The Brides of Garryowen.

---

☞MONDAY NEXT, MARCH 28, For Positively One Week Only,

## SUIL A MOR, ("The O'Dowd,")

AND

CLOSE OF Mr. BOUCICAULT'S ENGAGEMENT.

Manager for Mr. Dion Boucicault................Mr. H. J. Sargent

☞MONDAY, APRIL 4th—Mr. Boucicault's Great Play,

## JEANIE DEANS;

Or, THE HEART OF MID LOTHIAN,

for its first production here in twenty years.

FAST DAY—JEANIE DEANS MATINEE AT 2!

### N. Y. GERMANIA THEATRE COMPANY.

☞THE NEXT "FASHIONABLE EVENT,"—Herr Neuendorf's celebrated company from the Germania Theatre, New York, will appear at the Boston Museum the week of April 18th next, for five evenings and one matinee only.—*Gazette.*

The répertoire of plays to be produced is as follows:

Monday, April 18—DIE JOURNALISTEN.
Tuesday, April 19— EIN LUSTSPIEL, ("Mrs. Walthrop's Boarders.")
Wednesday, April 20 — DOCTOR KLAUS, ("Dr. Clyde.")
Thursday, April 21—DAS GLAS WASSER, (Un Verre d'Eau.)
Friday, April 22—DOCTOR WESPE, ("Dr. Wespe.")
Saturday Afternoon, April 23 –MINNA VON BARNHELM.

Der Direktor des Boston Museum Theaters, Herr R. M. Field, hat die berühmte Neuendorf'sche Germania Theater-Gesellschaft für 6 Vorstellungen in Boston, vom 18. April ab, engagirt, und sollte jeder Deutsche dies Unternehmen unterstützen.

—New England Staaten Zeitung.

☞Tickets will be delivered to subscribers TUESDAY, March 22, from 9 A. M. to 5 P. M., at the Boston Museum, under the direction of a committee of the Orpheus Musical Society, and all tickets then remaining unsold will be for sale at the Coat-Room, Boston Museum, Monday, Tuesday, Thursday and Friday of each week, (Fast Day excepted,) from 11 A. M. to 12 M., until April 12th, after which time they will be for sale at the Box-Office as usual.

☞There will be performances upon a Chickering Grand Piano in THE FRONT HALL, previous to the play, and occasionally between-acts, and A GONG BELL sounds there, previous to the commencement of each act.

☞Copies of Steel Engraving of Mr. Warren for sale at the Coat Room.

STAGE MANAGER ................................MR. WM. SEYMOUR
TREASURER................................MR. GEO. W. BLATCHFORD
BUSINESS AGENT................................MR. CYRUS A. PAGE

---

play after play, always, except perhaps in a gloomy production of Chekhov's "Ivanov" with Vivien Leigh, with unqualified success and public acceptance, Burton began to play Boston, too: in "Time Remembered," for one, co-starring with Helen Hayes; and in 1957 in the aforementioned "Camelot" with Miss Andrews (in which he acted with force and style and sang pretty dismally).

The two of them, Gielgud and Burton, came together again, this time in "Hamlet," with Gielgud as director and sepulchral voice of the unseen ghost, and Richard, of course, as the star. Unlike Gielgud's own Hamlet, which was conventional, this was presented on what was elaborately set up to suggest a bare stage, with the actors in rehearsal clothes. It attracted milling crowds to the Shubert in the two weeks beginning March 24, 1964, though there was some question, as Cheryl Crawford said, "whether they were coming to see Shakespeare's Hamlet or Taylor's Burton."

Burton had played Hamlet with the Old Vic company twelve years earlier at the Edinburgh Festival and in London and, in such scenes as that in which Hamlet berates his mother, very touching because of his boyishness. He had been no longer boyish, and although his performance was powerful, at times quite moving, it lacked the poetic qualities of Gielgud's.

Another English Hamlet in a period when we have had to rely on London actors to give us a chance at that great play, Maurice Evans appeared here after World War II in his "GI" version, which used sidearms and other explosive devices, and, for all its circus-like qualities, seemed brilliantly exciting. Mr. Evans, who never would be knighted because he became an American citizen in 1941, has acted in Boston time and again in

*Fanny Kemble (from the portrait by Thomas Sully), member of a great English acting dynasty. When she first played here, co-starring with her handsome father, the gentlemen of Boston were overwhelmed—a very rare thing in this vicinity.*

classic and modern roles, following in his own way the pattern of the old English stars: as Romeo, making his first U.S. performances to Katharine Cornell's Juliet at the Shubert opening November 4, 1935; as a brilliantly effete, elegant and eloquent King Richard II at the Boston Opera House two years later; as Falstaff; as Malvolio (with Helen Hayes as Viola) in "Twelfth Night"; in a full length "Hamlet"; and, with ease, assurance, and high comic style in one of his smoothest performances, as John Tanner in "Man and Superman," which ran for two happy weeks at the Shubert opening September 22, 1947.

Except for Dame Edith Evans, whom we missed, all the other stars of the British stage have been here in these latter years: Dame Sybil Thorndike,

*opposite: Dion Boucicault, popular Irish actor and playwright, appeared in his own "The Colleen Bawn" at the Boston Museum during the "31st week of the 40th season" of that famous playhouse.*

for example, in John Van Druten's "The Distaff Side" at the Shubert in 1935; Sir Cedric Hardwicke in "Shadow and Substance" at the Wilbur; Rex Harrison, with Lilli Palmer at the Plymouth in "Bell, Book, and Candle," and more recently in Pirandello's "Henry IV"; Paul Scofield with Alec McCowen as the fool and, as Cordelia, Diana Rigg, in the Royal Shakespeare Company's bizarre but brilliant "King Lear" in 1964; and, of course, Olivier.

Sir Laurence made his first Boston appearance in what was in some ways his most adventurous role, as Archie Rice in John Osborne's "The Entertainer." He had done it in London; he opened it here at our Shubert on January 28, 1958, in a stunning performance, beginning a whole new phase of his career. Here he was, the greatest classic actor of the world, dressed in a flashy cheap suit, a bowler hat too far over on one side of his head, a phony grin on his face, playing the saddest kind of unsuccessful music-hall performer—Archie Rice, who never made it as an actor or as a man, and who, God help him, knows it.

Some Bostonians were puzzled by Archie. When he danced badly and told Archie's awful jokes in a vaudeville sequence, they didn't know what to do. Here was a great actor, yet he seemed rather awful. But he *was* a star and a visitor. When he made his exit after that terrible vaudeville turn, they felt called upon to applaud, which they did feebly. Being sensitive to audience sounds and feelings, Sir Larry grinned a little, and the next night arranged the end of one scene so that none of those who were afraid of seeming inhospitable would be embarrassed: there was no room for applause. He went on from there in a perfect performance, deadly accurate, unsparing in its exposure of Archie's dreadful incompetence, rowdily comical with broadly bawdy jokes, and ultimately heartbreaking: one of the greatest performances, and surely the most misunderstood and underrated, by the greatest actor of our time.

He was back again, this time at the Colonial Theater, in March 1961 in Jean Anouilh's "Becket," in a rare and bold role-switch. In New York,

*The great Ellen Terry, an actress of independent spirit. Bernard Shaw wrote love letters to her for five years, while remaining faithful, of course, to his wife.*

with Anthony Quinn playing King Henry II, he had appeared in the title part, an elusive and secretive Becket, confidant of the King yet not confiding, fascinating, unfathomable, infuriating to the proud Henry. In Boston, for the first time he took over as Henry, giving the Becket role to Arthur Kennedy.

He had endowed Becket with a richness of personality that Kennedy, a fine actor, couldn't begin to achieve; and for the king, he would carry perplexity to outrage in a howling fit of anger that left him at one point rolling on the floor for just as long as it takes to read the words. Like so many of Olivier's performances, this was spectacular. He said later in an interview that "perhaps he had carried that particular scene too far." He hadn't: his Henry might have behaved in just that way.

During the last twenty years, the British have

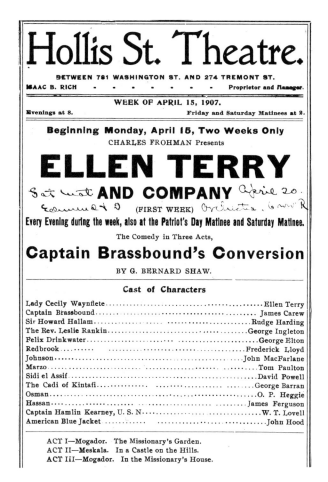

# Hollis St. Theatre.

**BETWEEN 781 WASHINGTON ST. AND 274 TREMONT ST.**

**ISAAC B. RICH** - - - - - - **Proprietor and Manager.**

### WEEK OF APRIL 15, 1907.

Evenings at 8.                    Friday and Saturday Matinees at 2.

### Beginning Monday, April 15, Two Weeks Only
CHARLES FROHMAN Presents

# ELLEN TERRY
## AND COMPANY
(FIRST WEEK)

Every Evening during the week, also at the Patriot's Day Matinee and Saturday Matinee.

The Comedy in Three Acts,

## Captain Brassbound's Conversion
BY G. BERNARD SHAW.

### Cast of Characters

Lady Cecily Waynflete.................................................Ellen Terry
Captain Brassbound................................................ James Carew
Sir Howard Hallam.................................................Rudge Harding
The Rev. Leslie Rankin.............................................George Ingleton
Felix Drinkwater...................................................George Elton
Redbrook.......................................................Frederick Lloyd
Johnson.......................................................John MacFarlane
Marzo...........................................................Tom Paulton
Sidi el Assif....................................................David Powell
The Cadi of Kintafi..............................................George Barran
Osman...........................................................O. P. Heggie
Hassan.........................................................James Ferguson
Captain Hamlin Kearney, U. S. N.................................W. T. Lovell
American Blue Jacket.............................................John Hood

ACT I—Mogador.  The Missionary's Garden.
ACT II—Meskala.  In a Castle on the Hills.
ACT III—Mogador.  In the Missionary's House.

*Program of the Hollis Street Theater for the week of April 15, 1907, when Ellen Terry starred in "Captain Brassbound's Conversion."*

sent us not only their stars but most of their best productions, with or without stars, and both of their great national acting companies. In most instances, as with the Royal Shakespeare Company's "King Lear" and "The Comedy of Errors" in 1964, they have favored Boston over all other cities except New York.

The R.S.C. brought us two of Harold Pinter's plays, creating a stir of excitement and some quiet puzzlement. Pinter's "The Caretaker," at the Wilbur with Alan Bates in 1961, and "The Homecoming" five years later at the Colonial, were new enough in form to annoy Bostonians who had expected conservative drama, and the later play

actually roused some of the old Puritan feeling among playgoers who had thought Puritanism was dead, or at least that they did not share its strictures. When the professor left his wife at the end with no more than a brief goodbye, knowing full well that she was remaining behind with his own disreputable family as a willing prostitute, there was no clucking of tongues: Bostonians do not cluck. But there was some quiet disapproval in the lobby of the Colonial.

Another Royal Shakespeare Company production was royally received here but it too, sad to say, caused a certain amount of bewilderment. This was Peter Brook's version of "A Midsummer's Night Dream," which turned Shakespeare's enchanted forest into a gymnasium. Every Boston playgoer agreed that it was enchanting, but some said rather firmly that they would have preferred the forest. If there was some regret about that gymnasium, however, there was much admiration for the production's adherence to Shakespeare's truth and Shakespeare's lines, which differentiated it from Mr. Brook's "King Lear" of 1964. In that, to make his (and Jan Kott's) point that Shakespeare was here exhibiting a totally bleak and pessimistic view of life, he had excised scenes and lines, twisting the tale.

If there was bewilderment over that "Dream," it was nothing compared to that on the opening night in 1969 of another classical British production, the "Hamlet" of Nicol Williamson. Having got along handsomely at the Colonial Theater as a somewhat sulky Prince, Mr. Williamson decided suddenly during the play-within-a-play that he was not acting as well as he might. So, while a puzzled audience stared, he stood up, threw down the golden goblet he had been holding, and walked off the stage muttering that he "couldn't go on with it any longer." Constance Cummings, as the Queen, recovered first; she came downstage to tell playgoers that the star was ill, which he was not. It was twenty long minutes before the star returned, apologized, insisted he had not been giving a good performance "whatever the critics might say to the contrary," but if everyone felt he should do so he

would pick up where he had left off and go on from there. Everyone felt he should continue, so he did, as if nothing untoward had happened. A good, at times brilliant, Hamlet, when he felt like it.

Another Briton, Dame Judith Anderson, elected to play Hamlet here not long after, following a tradition of actresses like Sarah Bernhardt. She did not walk off the stage during her single performance at Symphony Hall, but perhaps she might

have been advised to do so—or to have stayed off altogether. A chunky, spunky lady of seventy, she created none of the illusion of the young Hamlet and all but obliterated memories of her earlier greatness in the "Medea" of Robinson Jeffers, as Olga in Katharine Cornell's "The Three Sisters," the Queen in Gielgud's Hamlet" and, away back in 1929 in nearby Quincy, as Nina Leeds in the Boston-banned "Strange Interlude."

*Shylock was one of the great roles in Henry Irving's repertory.*

*Johnston Forbes-Robertson, one of England's great stars and one of the first to be knighted.*

# CHAPTER IV
## THE CONTINENTALS...

Continental stars followed the British to Boston and New York, eager for American commendation and for the Yankee dollar, too. Praise they solicited; money they loved. One of the most brilliant of them all, the Frenchwoman Sarah Bernhardt, insisted on being paid in gold, lots and lots of gold, during a series of cross-country excursions, the last five of which were advertised as "farewell tours." In the time of her life, very few stars were paid in bullion, but most great ladies of the stage were allowed to say goodbye, tearfully, more than once; it went with the territory.

Madame Sarah acted here in French, her own and only language, supported by Parisian players of her own choice, some of whom were very good indeed. On April 15, 1891, for example, when she began a two-week engagement at the Boston Theater in a repertory that included "L'Aiglon," "Tosca," "La Dame aux Camellias," and "Cyrano de Bergerac," her co-star was Constant Coquelin, for whom Edmond Rostand had written "Cyrano." Coquelin was as great an artist as she. Other Europeans offered themselves and their works on our stages in their own tongues, providing spectacular experiences for Bostonians who were multilingual and, if they were brilliant enough, an interesting one for those theater buffs who were anxious to watch them under no greater handicap than that of theatergoers who patronize operas in foreign languages. The magnificent Italian, Eleanora Duse, whose "natural" style of acting contrasted with the flamboyance of Bernhardt, played here in Italian down through the years until 1923, when she made her last appearances at the Boston Opera House in "Cosi Sia" and Ibsen's "Ghosts" on the final tour of her life: she died two weeks later in Pittsburgh.

Rachel, who was stately and grand, preceded Bernhardt in the long parade of French; she played the classics of the Paris repertory at the Boston Theater in 1855; her reputation was so great that top prices were raised to three dollars, and playgoers were warned against speculators who might get much more. In the week beginning October 22, following the traditional style of the great stars, she acted in a repertory of five plays, including the seventeenth century classics "Horace" and "Phedre," the ultimate tests of a French tragedienne's power, and, among others, "Adrienne Lecouvreur," which all audiences could weep over. Forty years later, another great lady of the Paris stage, Rejane, was welcomed at the Tremont in "Madame Sans Gene," a melodrama that stirred many actresses in an era when melodrama delighted almost everyone.

From Italy, Tomasso Salvini thundered into Boston to create a turmoil of admiration and wonder by his dramatic power, which was so formidable that when he played Othello his Desdemonas cowered in their stage beds for fear of strangulation. When he made his first appearance here, at the Boston Theater in November 1873, Tomasso was apparently insecure because of the language barrier, so he played in Italian with a company of players from home. Twelve years later, having learned no English but having acquired more courage, he acted at the Boston in Italian with a company whose other members, save only his son, Alexander, were all Americans, speaking English. In the spring of 1885, he created a sensation by appearing with the greatest American star, Edwin Booth, in "Othello" and in "Hamlet," in the title role of the first, as the ghost in the other; he in Italian, Booth and all the others in mellifluous

*The flamboyant and beautiful Sarah Bernhardt, one of the two greatest actresses of her day. The other was Eleanora Duse.*

Boston. Her leading man at the Globe, Orlando to her Rosalind at the time and during several of the years that followed, was Maurice Barrymore, who subsequently wrote for her a controversial drama entitled "Nadjezda."

Maurice, who would rather have been a playwright than an actor, was greatly enamored of "Nadjezda." Mme. Modjeska was intensely and passionately enamored of Maurice. Maurice toured with Madame, traveling from city to city in her elegant private railroad car, "Poland," sometimes along with his wife, Georgie Drew, and at least once with their son Lionel, then five, and their three-year-old daughter, Ethel. (Their youngest, John Barrymore, was left behind in Philadelphia with Grandma, Mrs. John Drew.) Modjeska and Georgie Drew Barrymore were rivals for the affections of the outrageously handsome Maurice, yet friends, too. It was Madame's influence that led Georgie to have her children baptized into the Catholic faith, despite the fierce opposition of Grandma Drew.

Georgie was an excellent comedienne, and a high-spirited wife, alert to all danger signs. In Boston on another tour, four years after that first appearance at the Globe, when it became obvious that Madame was getting pretty feverish about "Barry," Georgie gave her a hint, onstage, to keep hands off, and created an uproar. This was in "As You Like It" again, with Modjeska as heavenly Rosalind, Maurice as Orlando, and Georgie playing Celia, the confidant of Rosalind. In a scene in which Rosalind confesses to "sighing" for Orlando, the star's personal feelings became so apparent that Georgie invented a line to warn her: "Be sure 'tis but sighing you do," she warned, "lest it lead to deeper things."

According to James Kotsilibas-Davis, who tells the story in *Great Times, Good Times,* Madame Modjeska raged on the stage and all the way up into the flies, and took revenge by announcing she would play Barry's "Nadjezda" only at Wednesday matinees. That didn't bother Georgie. Since she

opposite: *Sarah Bernhardt.*

English. And so great was the understanding of the audiences at the Boston Theater that nobody seemed in the least puzzled when the spirit of Hamlet's father told his distraught son the true story of his murder in Italian. If Hamlet is a Dane speaking in English, why shouldn't his father converse with him in Italian?

The Polish exile Helena Modjeska, who had settled in California, spoke our language with a piquant accent not only comprehensible but charming when she played Rosalind in "As You Like It" at the Globe in 1880, opening a national tour, one of many that would bring her back to

A SARAH BERNHARDT

JULES BASTIEN·LEPAGE 1879

The Wm. Bourne & Son Piano Pronounced by the Musical World as The Best. 666 Washington Street, Boston.

# THE GLOBE THEATRE PROGRAMME

JAMES B. McALOON & CO., CUSTOM TAILORS, BOWDOIN SQUARE, BOSTON.

NEW ENGLAND CABINET ORGANS, SUPREME FAVORITES IN 1880, 1299 WASHINGTON ST., BOSTON.

## GLOBE THEATRE

PROPRIETOR AND MANAGER........................................MR. JOHN STETSON.

ENGAGEMENT OF

## SARAH BERNHARDT

MONDAY EVENING. DEC. 6th, 1880,

WILL BE PRESENTED

# HERNANI

A TRAGEDY IN FIVE ACTS, by VICTOR HUGO.

### CAST.

HERNANI........................................M. ANGELO
DON CARLOS........................................M. GANGLOFF
DON RUY GOMEZ DE SILVA........................................M. BOUILLOUD
DON SANCHO........................................M DORSAY
DON MATHIAS........................................M. DELETRAZ
DON RICARDO........................................M. THEFER
DON GARCIE........................................M. FOLLIET
UN MONTAGNARD........................................M. PIRON
DONNA JOSEFA........................................MME. MEA
JACQUEZ........................................M'LLE CARPENTIER
**DONA SOL........................................M'LLE SARAH BERNHARDT**

### REPERTOIRE FIRST WEEK.

TUESDAY........................................FROU-FROU
WEDNESDAY........................................ADRIENNE
THURSDAY........................................SPHINX
FRIDAY........................................PHEDRE
SATURDAY MATINEE........................................FROU-FROU

*The only Correct and Authorized Librettos of M'lle Bernhardt's Plays are those published by Mr. F. Rullman, Broadway, N.Y., and translated by Mr. F. A. Schwab, Acting Manager for Mr. H. E. Abbey. They are illustrated from designs made expressly by M'lle Bernhardt, and their genuineness is certified to by the artist's autograph signature. Price, 25 Cents. For sale in the lobby of the Theatre, and at Schornhof's, 146 Tremont Street.*

During the evening the Orchestra will perform the "Quand Meme March," (A. Spencer,) dedicated to M'lle Bernhardt.
CONDUCTOR........................................Mr. J. C. MULLALY

### SCALE OF PRICES.

GENERAL ADMISSION TO ALL PARTS OF THE HOUSE................ONE DOLLAR AND FIFTY CENTS

| | | |
|---|---|---|
| Orchestra Chairs, entire..........$3.00 | Balcony Centre Chairs..........$3.00 | Family Circle..........$1.00 |
| Orchestra Circle Chairs..........$3.00 | Balcony Sides..........$3.00 | Balcony Boxes, (Seating 6 Persons)..$15 & $20 |
| Balcony Circle, (Two Front Rows.)....$3.00 | Second Balcony..........$2.00 | Sofa Chairs..........$5.00 |

Proscenium Boxes........................................$15, $20 and $30, according to location

☞ Celebrated Weber Pianos used at this Theatre. Geo. D. Russell, 126 Tremont Street, Agent.

Parties purchasing tickets during the day will add greatly to their convenience by entering in the evening from Essex Street.

OPERA GLASSES TO LET IN THE LOBBY. CARRIAGES may be called at the Essex or Washington Street Entrance.

SMOKING ROOM.—Located over the Washington St. entrance; enter head of stairway leading to the balcony.

## GLOBE THEATRE.

The Most Magnificent Theatre in America!

No Theatre in the City Equals this for Sterling Attractions!

**Monday. Dec. 6,**
The Fashionable attraction of the year,
**SARAH BERNHARDT**
For Twelve Performances only.

GRAND NOVELTY FOR
Christmas & New Years
**HOLIDAYS**
Commencing
Monday, Dec. 20th,
**KIRALFY BROS.'**
Majestic Spectacle,
**ENCHANTMENT**
WITH ITS
Grand Ballet & World of Novelties.

**Monday. Jan. 3.**
For Two Weeks only,
THE ARTISTIC SUCCESS OF THE SEASON
Farewell Engagement
Of the Eminent Italian Tragedian,
**SALVINI**
SUPPORTED BY
AN AMERICAN COMPANY
Signor Salvini's American Tour extends Five Months, under the management of Mr. John Stetson.

**Mrs. SCOTT SIDDONS**
Supported by her own Dramatic Company.
EMMA ABBOTT'S OPERA TROUPE.
The Famous
**SALSBURY'S TROUBADOURS**
The inimitable, the original and only
**VOKES FAMILY,**
Commencing an American Engagement of six months, under the management of Mr. John Stetson.

Other Celebrities
Are engaged and will be duly announced.

owned the rights to the play, she went into U.S. District Court in Boston and sued for an injunction. Although Modjeska had her way with the play, she didn't have her way with Maurice, and eventually Judge Lowell decided that Georgie was entitled to have "Nadjezda" put on when she so desired. Everyone cooled off after that.

Modjeska was still playing Rosalind at forty-five, which sounds a little grim at this remove in time, but she was universally accepted in this and most other roles as a great actress.

Bernhardt was just as temperamental as Modjeska and far more flamboyant. Even in her old age, when she continued to tour the United States though she was now a cripple, one of her legs amputated, she made news by her words offstage and on. She played the Globe in Boston for the first time in 1880, and dazzled everyone in "Adrienne Lecouvreur," in "Phedre," in "Froufrou," and in "La Dame aux Camellias," her most spectacular showpiece. Back at the Hotel Vendome on Commonwealth Avenue, in stunts on the Charles River, and at Longfellow's home in Cambridge she made news.

Longfellow wasn't in the habit of entertaining actresses, and when Sarah asked to come and see him he insisted he had another engagement. But she persisted: he was her favorite poet, and his "Hiawatha," which according to Cornelia Otis Skinner, her biographer, she pronounced "Eehah-vah-ta," was her favorite poem. So the poet of Brattle Street summoned William Dean Howells, a real theater buff and playwright, and Dr. Oliver Wendell Holmes as chaperones, and was, of course, charmed. She had wanted, she exclaimed in her fragmented English, to do a bust of him—sculpture was one of her hobbies—but mostly to admire him. The bust he set aside, the admiration he accepted. On leaving his house, the exuberant Sarah threw her arms around the benign poet and

*opposite: Sarah Bernhardt was snubbed in some cities during the first of her many American tours, but Bostonians crowded into the Globe Theater on Washington Street, near Essex, when she played there in 1880.*

kissed him, exclaiming the while with Bernhardtian fervor, "Ah, que je vous admire!" If you walk along Brattle Street now, pausing in front of the Longfellow House, you may still hear a soft rustle, a dim distant echo of the shock that ran through Cambridge on that occasion.

Eleanora Duse, who made her first appearances at the Boston Theater in April 1896, was the exact opposite of Bernhardt in all ways. Where the Frenchwoman was outgoing, explosive, positive, she kept to herself. Onstage, Sarah performed, Duse lived her roles, or seemed to. Sarah was a mistress of stage techniques and tricks, brilliant

*Helena Modjeska. European-born, she toured America often and played Boston with Maurice Barrymore, whose wife was jealous.*

*Rejane, born Gabrielle Reju, one of the greatest French actresses. She died in 1920.*

and endearing. Duse's acting was simple, stark, and even when one didn't know either the play or her language, as when she gave a matinee of "Cosi Sia" at the Opera House in 1923, almost awesome to watch because of something mysteriously fascinating in her personality and something profoundly affecting in the simplicity of her performance.

Thirty years before "Cosi Sia" and "Ghosts," her last plays in Boston, she had appeared in a repertory that included "Camille," "La Locanderia," "Fedora," and "Cavalleria Rusticana" at the Globe. Bostonians were fascinated and even astonished by her combination of power and personal appeal. Back for another visit in October 1902, she so stirred Amy Lowell that Amy followed her to Philadelphia; she became "the overwhelming vision" that started Amy writing poetry.

On Bernhardt's first visit to Boston, she was accompanied by a retinue of two maids, two cooks, a maitre d', and her personal secretary, all paid by her producers, who guaranteed her a minimum of $1,000 per performance for one hundred performances. Duse traveled anonymously, wore no makeup on or offstage, didn't bother to tint her gray hair. Both were admired by Bostonians, though not necessarily the same Bostonians.

The Irish sent over individual players of reputation and, in 1911, to open their first tour of America, the great Abbey Theater Company of Dublin, with its two founders, William Butler Yeats and Lady Gregory, and an ensemble that impressed the Boston *Transcript* critic, Henry Taylor Parker. He declared that "no company within Boston memory has so played as a team." At the Plymouth Theater, which they opened in an atmosphere that was somewhat tense because some members of Boston's Irish community were hostile, the Abbey players put on John Millington Synge's "In the Shadow of the Glen," Lady Gregory's "Hyacinth Halvey" and "Spreading the News," "Birthright" by T. C. Murray, and, among other fresh and brilliant dramas, the controversial "Playboy of the Western World."

Written by Synge, "Playboy" was considered potentially explosive. Back in Dublin it had caused a riot in the Abbey, reportedly because of a bit of dialogue in which one character uses the word "shift," meaning petticoat. No Irishwoman, said the dissenters, would ever speak in such wicked terms. Because there were rumblings that something untoward might happen when "Playboy" was presented at the Plymouth, Professor George Pierce Baker of Harvard stationed some of his students of English 47 in key seats about the theater with orders to report to him any signs of potential trouble. Wisner Kinne, the biographer of Baker, remembers that the professor himself sighted one possible miscreant acting restlessly in an aisle seat

opposite: *Eleanora Duse.*

and personally escorted him out onto Stuart Street. Despite some fanciful accounts to the contrary, there was no more trouble. The Abbey Company was a hit in Boston.

In 1923, the Soviet Union sent over its proudest and most famous players, the Moscow Art Company, to act for a week in Russian at the Opera House. Founded in Czarist times by Constantin Stanislavsky and Vladimir Nemirovich-Danchenko, the Moscow Art had not only survived the Revolution but had been adopted by the Soviet state. Stanislavsky had not only discovered Anton Chekhov, Russia's greatest dramatist, but had developed extraordinary new methods of directing and of training actors. His "method" would become, as it is today in New York and Hollywood, the universally favored system of instruction in acting.

At the Boston Opera House, during the week beginning December 31, 1923, Stanislavsky was one of the actors who appeared in Goldoni's "The Mistress of the Inn," Chekhov's "Ivanov" and "The Cherry Orchard"; in Gorki's "The Lower Depths," along with Ibsen's "An Enemy of the People"; a version of "The Brothers Karamazov," and a drama called "In the Claws of Life."

The Moscow Art Theater has never returned to Boston, but the Abbey has been back many times, most recently in 1977 with Sean O'Casey's "The Plough and the Stars"; and various other national European troupes, including Marcel Marceau, the mime, and the Kabuki of Japan, have been accepted and welcomed. Our playgoers are not only discerning, but also hospitable.

opposite: *The great Eleanora Duse's last Boston appearances were given at the Boston Opera House, in Italian, in 1923. She played in "Cosi Sia" and Ibsen's "Ghosts." A few weeks later she died, in Pittsburgh.*

overleaf and following: *The Conscience of the King—Hamlet in Boston.*

# BOSTON OPERA HOUSE

LEE & J. J. SHUBERT, Proprietors

L. H. MUDGETT, Manager

---

## F. RAY COMSTOCK and MORRIS GEST

Have the Great Honor of Presenting

*The World's Greatest Tragedienne*

# ELEONORA DUSE

and Her Company from Rome

*For a Limited Engagement of Two Matinees*

at the

## BOSTON OPERA HOUSE

Only Appearance in New England

---

## Thursday Matinee, December 6th

—in—

# "COSI SIA"

## "THY WILL BE DONE"

A Drama in Three Acts

### By COUNT TOMMASO GALLARATI-SCOTTI

### CAST OF CHARACTERS

THE MOTHER—A simple, trustful, devout soul, whose whole life is wrapped up in her boy. The epitome of motherhood in all ages.　　　　　　　　　　　　　　　　　　　　ELEONORA DUSE

GIOVANNI, THE SON—A child at the point of death in the first act. A handsome, carefree, selfish young man of the world thereafter, seeker of the joys of life; ashamed of his Mother and indifferent to her affection.　　　　　　　　　　　　　　　　　　　　MEMO BENASSI

ANGELA—A friend of the Mother's, who consoles her in her grief and urges her to pray to the Virgin.　　　　　　　　　　　　　　　　　　　　IONE MORINO

SIMONE, THE FATHER—A blunt, feelingless peasant, unable to comprehend his wife's devotion and tenderness for her son. Giovanni inherits from him his selfish and care-free character.　　LEO ORLANDINI

THE DOCTOR—A typical country physician, who recognizes no powers beyond those of his craft, and gives up the child's case as hopeless.　　　　　　　　　　　　　　　ALFREDO ROBERT

ANDREOTTO, THE VETERINARY—A boon companion of Simone, who sympathizes with the Mother, in his crude way, as she climbs the Mount of the Crosses.　　　　　　　　　CIRO GALVANI

ONORIO—The druggist, a young man, a friend of Giovanni's.　　　　　　　GINO FANTONI

LUCA—The baker's son, another friend of Giovanni's.　　　　　　　　LUIGI COLAVITTI

ALVINA—A young girl in whom Giovanni, the son, is interested.　　　　　ENIF ROBERT

GEMMA—Another young girl in Giovanni's group of friends.　　　　　　MARIA MORINO

MARINA—Another young girl in Giovanni's group of friends.　　　　　　IONE MORINO

THE BLIND ONE—A mendicant, seeking alms on the Mount of the Crosses.　　MARIO GALLI

THE CRIPPLE—Another mendicant.　　　　　　　　　　　　　ALFREDO ROBERT

THE SACRISTAN—Keeper of the Chapel of the Miracles.　　　　　　　LEO ORLANDINI

*Henry Irving as Hamlet.*

*Edwin Forrest, first American star, as Hamlet.*

*Edwin Booth as Hamlet.*

# MAURICE EVANS

*Presents His*

## TWO 1939 TRIUMPHS

DIRECT FROM ST. JAMES' THEATRE, NEW YORK

SHAKESPEARE'S

# HAMLET IN ITS ENTIRETY

**NIGHTLY**
Except
Wed. and Sat.
at
7 p.m. (to 11:15)

**MATINEES**
Wed. & Sat.
at
1 p.m. (to 5:15)

THE FIRST PART OF

SHAKESPEARE'S HISTORICAL COMEDY

**ONLY**
2 PERFORMANCES
WEEKLY

# HENRY IV

WED. & SAT.
EVENINGS
at 8:30 P.M.

*with* MR. EVANS *as* FALSTAFF

*Maurice Evans as Hamlet.*

*John Gielgud and Judith Anderson as Hamlet and Queen Gertrude, at the Shubert Theater in 1937.*

*Leslie Howard as Hamlet.*

JOHN
BARRYMORE
as
"HAMLET"
FRANCIS BRUGUIERE
—PHOTO—

*John Barrymore as Hamlet.*

opposite: *Program of Judith Anderson's one performance at Symphony Hall, February 5, 1971. She wasn't good.*

*Richard Burton was a Hamlet.*

*Nicol Williamson, the English star, played Hamlet at the Colonial Theater in 1971 and startled Bostonians by walking off stage during the first night performance.*

CHARLOTTE AND SUSAN CUSHMAN
AS
ROMEO AND JULIET.
ACT 2. SCENE 2.

# CHAPTER V

## ...AND, OF COURSE, THE AMERICANS

When the first American stars appeared in Boston, they followed the patterns established by their British predecessors and rivals. They proved their right to stardom by playing grandly the great classic roles, principally those of Shakespeare's most popular plays, presenting four or five in repertory during engagements of a week or two, or perhaps three. Like the British, the men had to prove they were great in "King Richard III"; in "Hamlet"; in "Othello" as the hero and also as his villainous conspirator, Iago; in "Macbeth," and in "King Lear." For the ladies, it was necessary to play Juliet sweetly and Lady Macbeth ferociously. So they all did.

When Edwin Forrest, a native Philadelphian, acted at the old Federal Street Theater on February 5, 1827, to prove to the discriminating Boston audience that he was a true star—the first American to deserve that title—he took the leading roles in six plays, including "Othello," "King Lear" (which was quite a challenge for an actor then only twenty-one years old), "King Richard III," and one of his own favorites, "Damon and Pythias," in which he was Pythias, and by common consensus quite wonderful.

Edwin Booth, who had made his professional stage debut at the Boston Museum in 1849 supporting his erratic father, Junius, in the tiny role of Tressel in "King Richard III," came back to Boston eight years later to make his first bid for stardom. He, too, followed the British system, as he would down through the years in many, many Boston appearances. During the two weeks beginning

April 20, 1857, at the Boston Theater, Edwin played Sir Giles Overreach in "A New Way to Pay Old Debts" by Massinger, such newer favorites as "Brutus" by John Howard Payne (author of "Home Sweet Home"), and acted, too, in "Hamlet" and (at the age of twenty-three) "King Lear." Although some Boston reviewers in that benighted era were puzzled by the modest quietness of his "Hamlet," he was successful. A year later, in the same huge playhouse, he stayed three weeks instead of two and added, for the first time in Boston, "Macbeth" and "Romeo and Juliet." His Juliet, parenthetically, was Mary Devlin, whom he married two years later and with whom he lived for two months in a house on Washington Street, Dorchester, where she died on February 20, 1863. She is buried at Mt. Auburn Cemetery, where his body lies too.

In the meantime, the first of our great ladies, Charlotte Cushman, who had started her career at eighteen in the Tremont Theater as an opera singer, had become a stage star overnight by a prodigious performance as Lady Macbeth in New Orleans on April 23, 1836, a performance in which she was described as "a pantheress let loose" and "first cousin to Medea." Like the men, she adhered to the classical repertory as the essence and basis of her acting, with, of course, her own kind of transvestism (a word nobody knew back in those benighted days). She was conventional, if overpowering, as Lady Macbeth. But she switched sexes to play Romeo, too.

In her Boston acting debut at the Tremont Theater in 1837, she "amazed the town" as Portia, as Lady Macbeth, and as obstreperous Lady Gay Spanker in Boucicault's "London Assurance." When she came back in 1858 at the Boston Theater

*opposite: Charlotte Cushman as Romeo, with her sister Susan, as Juliet.*

*Edwin Forrest of Philadelphia, first American star, in his most popular role as "Metamora," a character modeled after the Wampanoag Indian chief, King Philip.*

those of Shakespeare, considering it their cultural duty to keep these dramas alive in the theater and their professional opportunity to exhibit themselves in the greatest roles ever devised by any dramatist. Robert Mantell, an Englishman who spent much of his career in the United States, played Boston in Shakespearean repertory for many years. So did Richard Mansfield, a native of Scotland, who came to the United States for the first time with Modjeska and stayed here as an American favorite. So, too, E. H. Sothern and Julia Marlowe, American co-stars much like the English couple Irving and Terry; they played Boston each year with the classic dramas in the old style.

*Maurice Barrymore, founder of the Barrymore-Drew dynasty, father of John, Ethel and Lionel.*

in what was advertised as a farewell performance before "her final retirement from the stage"—one of several farewell appearances she kept making during the next eighteen years—she not only played the ladies' roles in "She Stoops to Conquer" and "Macbeth" and "King Kenry VIII," but also Romeo, with Mary Devlin, Booth's future wife, as Juliet. Later, in London, her Juliet was her sister, Susan Cushman; in London, they loved Romeo and Susan.

Other American stars of the nineteenth and twentieth centuries followed these three great pioneers by keeping to the English tradition. They, too, played the star parts in the classic plays, especially

*Mrs. John Drew, matriarch of the Drew-Barrymore dynasty, in one of her most famous roles, as Mrs. Malaprop in "The Rivals."*

style that, alas, ended shortly afterward in New York.

In the meantime, some Americans began to abandon the classics in favor of lesser plays that might give them one good part, and to tour the country with full companies; this was far less expensive and less cumbersome than a big repertory. The old stock companies, which had supported Kean and the Booths and Charlotte Cushman in their tours of the country, began to shut down. That at the Boston Theater ended its career in 1885; eight years later, the Boston Museum gave up its stock policy. There would be other stock troupes here, like that at the Castle Square, for example, but they now played comedies and melodramas, changing bills usually each week, and performed with their own modest players and with stars.

Early in his career, Edwin Forrest had started the movement to new plays by offering prizes to

*Charlotte Cushman 1843.*

And we do not forget Walter Hampden, who appeared here with his own company year after year, playing "Cyrano de Bergerac" as a popular favorite, but almost always including Shakespeare, too. Thirty years ago, after a lifetime following the old classic procedure as his own manager, Hampden joined the American Repertory Theater of Eva Le Gallienne, Margaret Webster, and Cheryl Crawford, which opened in Boston at the Colonial Theater with Shakespeare's "The Tempest" as the centerpiece of a three-play repertory in the old

American writers and finding at least three that were often more popular than his "King Richard III," which he considered his *chef d'oeuvre*. In one of these, which was written by John Augustus Stone of Concord and which won Forrest's $500 prize in 1828, he played an Indian Chief called Metamora, who was modeled after the great and good leader of the Wampanoags, King Philip. In the text this is a bombastic melodrama, but Forrest acted "Metamora" for forty years with huge success in Boston and everywhere else.

Other classical actors became associated with similar showpieces, as the Englishman Henry Irving did with the melodrama called "The Bells." But while the superstars continued to remain loyal to Shakespeare, too, as an obligation and a matter of pride, some of the Americans found lesser dramas with which they could live comfortably for most of a lifetime. What happened with James O'Neill, father of Eugene, is typical.

O'Neill was a self-trained actor who, when he

was based in a Chicago stock company, had played opposite Booth in the kind of switch of which Booth was fond, alternating Othello and Iago, and had been praised by that star. He himself aspired to the same kind of greatness, but in 1883 he substituted in New York in a play based on the romantic novel "The Count of Monte Cristo" which became a popular hit of huge proportions. That changed his life.

Arthur and Barbara Gelb in their biography of Eugene O'Neill recall what happened to James: "'The Count of Monte Cristo,' which was to bring James the popularity and wealth for which he yearned . . . put a strict limitation on his career. It became the trap from which he never escaped." In "A Long Day's Journey into Night," see James Tyrone's lamentation to his son, Edmund, about

*Charlotte Cushman as Meg Merrilies, one of her most popular roles.*

*Charlotte Cushman ". . . as platform reader . . ." (1875)*

what a play he calls "The Bells" did to his career—keeping in mind that James Tyrone, Sr., is actually James O'Neill, that "The Bells" is actually "The Count of Monte Cristo," and that Edmund is really Eugene O'Neill himself.

Joseph Jefferson III didn't consider "Rip Van Winkle" a great comedown or a trap. Joe had been brought up in the British tradition as grandson of the first Joe Jefferson, whose father, Tom, had acted in London with David Garrick and had begun his American career in Boston in 1795 at the Federal Street Theater. But Joe III gave up almost everything else to play old Rip and one other character of somewhat greater literary standing, Bob Acres in Sheridan's "The Rivals." Joe appeared as Rip for the first time here at the Boston Theater, starting on May 3, 1869, for four weeks, a long run for a single play in those days. The records show he was back again in 1870 and 1871, and by that time the chroniclers were happily referring to his appearances as his "annual visit." Back he came almost every year, alternating sometimes as Bob Acres until May 11, 1901, by which time he had also added "The Cricket on the Hearth" and the farce "Lend Me Five Shillings" as afterpieces. They loved him at the Boston.

A popular star named Denman Thompson made his first appearance at the Boston in 1880 with a comedy of rural life as it might have been in another, more romantic world; it was called "Joshua Whitcomb." Six years later, he and George W. Ryer completed a sequel called "The Old Homestead," in which he continued the story of his hero in the town of Swanzey, N.H. The play was an old-fashioned antecedent of "Our Town" and Swanzey was a prototype of Thornton Wilder's Grover's Corners (which, of course, is modeled

*In the days when the Howard Athenaeum was respectable, Charlotte Cushman was one of its stars in "The School for Scandal." Note that a "comeditta" called "Ladies Beware" was also on the bill for September 10, 1850. This was an "afterpiece," something light for the light-minded. Note also that the "free list" was suspended, except, of course, for the press.*

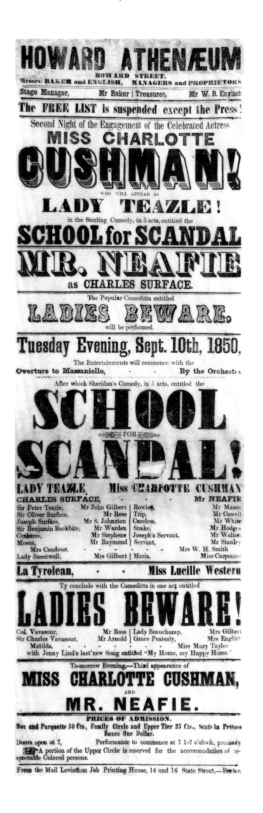

*Maude Adams in 1905 as Peter Pan.*

after Peterborough, N.H.). Like Joe Jefferson and Rip, Denman and "The Old Homestead" were beloved in Boston, playing here annually, always with great popularity, for a total of fifty weeks at the Boston Theater alone during the twenty-one years between the premiere and the final performance on February 23, 1901.

When the new Shubert Theater opened on January 24, 1910, the first attraction was an American repertory company following faithfully the old, honored British tradition. The co-stars were E. H. Sothern and Julia Marlowe; the plays, Shakespeare's "The Taming of the Shrew," "The Merchant of Venice," "Twelfth Night," "Romeo and Juliet," and, of course, "Hamlet." Eighteen months later, when the Plymouth Theater opened its doors for the first time on September 23, 1911, the actors

who were greeted officially by Mayor John F. Fitzgerald and his wife (accompanied by their daughter Rose, who would later become the mother of President John F. Kennedy) were members of a repertory company, too; the Abbey Theater of Dublin, making their first appearance on the American stage. But their repertory was different. Having no native tradition, these Irish actors had been creating their own classics, among them John Millington Synge's "The Playboy of the Western World," which they would give to the western world along with many others in a period when the theater was looking for and beginning to find new classics, more suited, perhaps, to the times, which were changing. By that time, a new generation of American stars like Maude Adams and Ethel Barrymore had begun their careers in New York and, having pleased the people there, had hastened to Boston, not in repertory and not in Shakespeare, either, but in single dramas by contemporary authors who would serve them and many others like them, here and across the country.

Miss Adams, a Mayflower descendant who had been brought up in such places as San Francisco and Salt Lake City, was held in the highest esteem by Bostonians and by Harvard men, who twice invited her to act in Cambridge. But although she got good reviews at the Boston Theater in "Romeo and Juliet" in 1899 and appeared at Sanders Theater in "Twelfth Night" for two performances nine years later, she made her reputation very largely in the sentimental comedies of James M. Barrie, a young Scotsman.

As Viola in "Twelfth Night" at Sanders Theater, she received a laurel wreath and a full-throated Harvard cheer. Later, in a spectacular version of Schiller's "The Maid of Orleans" at Harvard Stadium, she was even more spectacularly acclaimed. And at the end of her career, as an elderly lady, she went back to "Twelfth Night" in a lesser role, as Maria in a production that toured the summer theater, opening in Ogunquit, Maine, and gave her last performance on any stage on Saturday evening, September 8, 1934, at the Cape Playhouse in Dennis on Cape Cod.

Maude Adams became a star in Barrie's "The Little Minister," which she presented at the Hollis Street Theater for sixty-five performances beginning November 19, 1898. A year later, first in New York, then in Boston, and then everywhere else, she was elevated to the status of superstar in and as "Peter Pan." "The Little Minister" established her as a great American actress; "Peter Pan" made her a legend in her own time and a great name even in ours.

Ethel Barrymore, daughter of stars, niece of stars, sister and granddaughter of stars, might have been expected to follow in the grand tradition for she was trained in it: she had her first real education in the art of acting as a member of the London company of Henry Irving. But when Ethel came back to America, she found her first starring vehicle in a comedy by a young American named Clyde Fitch, a new man in town. The play, called "Captain Jinks of the Horse Marines," opened in Philadelphia, went on to enormous success in New York, and then to Boston in 1901, for the first time but not the last. Everybody loved her in "Captain Jinks"; every man fell in love with her, for she was very pretty.

Ethel was a star for more than forty years, and although she had a fling at Juliet in New York in 1922 and at Ophelia three years later, she stayed with the newer English, European, and American authors, including James M. Barrie, in whose "The Twelve Pound Look" she played here at B. F. Keith's vaudeville theater. Bred in the old tradition of acting, which was florid and often declamatory, she made the transition to the more modern style in newer dramas like Ibsen's "A Doll's House," and long before the end of a great career, in Boston in 1942 at the Wilbur as the schoolteacher in "The Corn Is Green" she had mastered the naturalistic technique. She was a great actress, and proved it without feeling the need to test herself in the old classic roles, except for two brief flings.

Most of the American stars of the twentieth century have followed the lead of Maude Adams and Ethel Barrymore, not that of Sothern and

*Maude Adams originated "Peter Pan," her greatest role, in New York, then brought it to Boston. Herewith the bill at the Hollis Street Theater, then our most fashionable playhouse, for November 5, 1906.*

Marlowe, or Walter Hampden, or the others who worked in the English classical tradition. Helen Hayes has played classic roles here and in other major cities; so has Katharine Hepburn, who has

*Joseph Jefferson in "Rip Van Winkle," a favorite in Boston and throughout the country for twenty years.*

Hollywood assignments to return, she made her reputation in modern dramas like Shaw's "Candida" and "Saint Joan" and in "The Barretts of Wimpole Street."

Let it be noted that she had a special feeling for Boston, and being her own producer, and therefore able to decide her own commitments, not only presented each of her productions here but made sure they were well-tested elsewhere; she never played Boston in a tryout. At the end of her extraordinary career, she appeared here in a two-character play by Jerome Kilty called "Dear Liar," which was based on the correspondence between George Bernard Shaw and the actress, Mrs. Patrick Campbell. On Saturday, May 7, 1960, she gave the last performance of her long career at the Wilbur.

The career of Helen Hayes has been oriented toward New York with some significant visits to Hollywood and an occasional foreign tour, but she has played Boston with almost every show over a long period of years, and always with unqualified

*Maude Adams as Joan of Arc in Schiller's "The Maid of Orleans" in Harvard Stadium, 1909. She was supported by a cast of 1400 including members of Boston's Battery A as the French cavalry.*

the courage to try anything she finds challenging. But Katharine Cornell, one of the greatest ladies of our American stage, appeared here only twice in classic roles: in 1934 in "Romeo and Juliet" with Maurice Evans at the Shubert Theater as one stop in a national tour, and eighteen years later at the same playhouse in "Antony and Cleopatra" with Godfrey Tearle and such young actors as Charlton Heston in small roles. Like most American actresses who stayed on the stage, or found time between

success; she is a particular favorite of our audiences. Miss Hayes has paid her dues to Shakespeare, as Viola and as Portia, and in a recital for two voices called "Shakespeare Revisited" with Maurice Evans. But she, too, has won the affection of our people in modern comedies and, perhaps most spectacularly, in the chronicle play "Victoria Regina."

The Hayes vehicles that have pleased Bostonians included "What Every Woman Knows" by James M. Barrie; the biographical "Harriet," in which she represented Harriet Beecher Stowe with particular grace and charm; and "Mrs. McThing," in which in 1942 she personated in her own impish comic style the happily addled Mrs. Howard V. LaRue II. There have been many more, including the tinkling duchess in Anouilh's "Time Remembered," and her first O'Neill, as the heartbreakingly loyal Nora Melody in "A Touch of the Poet" at the Colonial Theater in the fall of 1958.

Miss Hepburn, who established her independence of customs and annoying rules early in her career, has emerged from Hollywood time and again to act in popular comedies, in a musical comedy, and on several occasions in the great comic roles of Shakespeare: as Rosalind in "As You Like It," as Portia in "The Merchant of Venice," as Beatrice in "Much Ado About Nothing," as Viola in "Twelfth Night," and in a more serious vein, as Cleopatra in "Antony and Cleopatra." Most of these she originated at the American Shakespeare Festival Theater in Stratford, Conn., two she offered in Boston. We saw her here as Rosalind, for which her legs were too slenderly pretty—in the forest of Arden she would have been in danger of romantic assault—and as Beatrice, which suited her better. She is not always great in performance, being limited by her voice, but she is great on courage and loyalty to the theater.

Of the American men, what can we say except that most of them in the last fifty years have abandoned the old traditions, and the stage, too, for Hollywood and television. Spencer Tracy, one of the greatest, who could and should have played the classic roles—think of him as Macbeth!—estab-

*Edwin Booth, the greatest of all American actors.*

lished the pattern most of them have followed. He was snatched by a film scout from a play called "The Last Mile" in 1929 and didn't return till 1946, when he appeared in a drama by Robert E. Sherwood called "The Rugged Path" at the Plymouth Theater for two weeks, then in New York for a short run.

Kirk Douglas left the stage for Hollywood in the same way and didn't come back until 1963. On October 28, he opened at the Shubert in "One Flew Over the Cuckoo's Nest," in which he played one of the cuckoos. Not very impressive. Gregory Peck, very young then and even handsomer than he is now, acted at the Shubert during the week of November 30, 1942 in "The Willow and I." At that time, his ambition was to play Romeo, and he

would have made a great one. But he, too, went away to Hollywood and became an institution. Mr. Peck has made some attempts to break away, and for one week, twenty years ago, acted at the Cape Playhouse in Synge's "The Playboy of the Western World." But his playboy looked and sounded just like Gregory Peck, which is fine, except it has nothing to do with the play.

Henry Fonda has gone back and forth from New York to Hollywood and has duly played Boston with his hits. But Henry has avoided the classics,

*Otis Skinner played a hundred parts or more during a long career. He was most admired as the beggar Hajj in "Kismet."*

while his contemporaries in England—Olivier, Richardson, Gielgud, Guinness, O'Toole, Scofield, and the others—have made films too, and have done commercial plays, but have stretched themselves and stimulated their audiences and kept their obligation to the theater at its best by taking time out year after year to play the great classic roles. George C. Scott, one of the great American actors of the moment, played Shakespeare (Antony, Shylock, and Richard III) in his earlier career, though never in Boston. And he has had the courage to break away from Hollywood and television and to keep coming back to the stage in challenging roles; but those he has played here, except for Fox-

---

### THE CAPE PLAYHOUSE
Telephone Dennis 60
Evenings at 8:30 Matinees Wednesday and Friday at 2:45.
All Seats Reserved. No Sunday Performances.
Prices:—Evening 50c to $2.50, Matinees 50c to $2.00 (all plus tax).
Box Office open from 9:30 A.M. to 10 P.M. daily except Sunday.

**Beginning Monday Evening, September 3rd**

RAYMOND MOORE
Presents

## MAUDE ADAMS
With a Distinguished Company of Players
in

## "Twelfth Night"

A Whimsical Masque by William Shakespeare

**CAST**

ORSINO, Duke of Illyria .................... BRAM NOSSEN
SEBASTIAN, brother to Viola .......... FREDERICK PATTERSON
ANTONIO, a sea captain, friend to Sebastian ........ BYRON RUSSELL
VALENTINE ⎰ Gentlemen attending ........ LOUIS KRUGMAN
CURIO    ⎱ on the Duke ........ MAURICE LANCASTER
A SEA CAPTAIN, friend to Viola .......... EDGAR BARRIER
SIR TOBY BELCH .......... C. NORMAN HAMMOND
SIR ANDREW AGUECHEEK .......... CHARLES H. CROKER-KING
MALVOLIO, a steward to Olivia .......... FREDERICK ROLAND
FESTE, a clown, servant to Olivia .......... LE ROI OPERTI
FABIAN .......... EDGAR BARRIER
OLIVIA .......... CECILE WULFF
VIOLA .......... MARIE ADELS
MARIA .......... MAUDE ADAMS
GUESTS .......... GWEN ROSSITER and LUCY HORNER
A BOY .......... ALDON MacKAY
AN INNKEEPER .......... BERNARD FABRIZI
WILL SHAKESPEARE .......... EDGAR BARRIER
FIRST OFFICER .......... BERNARD FABRIZI
SECOND OFFICER .......... LOUIS KRUGMAN
BLUE BOYS .......... TED ASHERMAN and GIBBONS ASH

The action takes place in Illyria and is continuous except for one interval of ten minutes

Stage Manager, SAMUEL PEARCE

The production designed by DAVID S. GAITHER and executed under his supervision in the workshops of the MANHATTAN THEATRE COLONY at Ogunquit, Maine.

The whole production under the supervision of WALTER HARTWIG
Miss Adams' costume designed by MRS. JOHN W. ALEXANDER
The production costumes designed and executed by ELIZABETH STUART CLOSE of New York

---

*Playbill for Maude Adams's last show. The great American star made a summer tour as Maria in "Twelfth Night," opening September 3, 1934, and closing the following Saturday when she gave her final professional performance.*

well J. Sly in "Sly Fox," are out of the modern repertory. Foxwell is a modified version of old Ben Jonson's hero in "Volpone," acted with enormous gusto in the true classical style.

The three greatest American actors of the last one hundred and twenty-five years were Booth, Barrymore, and Brando. What they chose to do, in Boston and elsewhere, is typical; they set the styles.

Booth did not hesitate to act in contemporary plays; he was not priggish. But he did feel an obligation to the great plays as most English actors and continental actors do today. He not only played the roles that his audiences favored—Iago, for example—but all the others in the range of greatness. And he challenged his major contemporaries: he acted with Lawrence Barrett, with

*Julia Marlowe as Juliet.*

*Robert Mantell, a star in the classical tradition.*

Charlotte Cushman, who at the time had a greater following than he, and with the wild Italian Salvini, exchanging roles from night to night.

John Barrymore, who respected Booth but simply did not bother to follow his example, made his professional debut in 1901 in a vaudeville act supporting his father, Maurice, at the Park Theater in Worcester, Mass., and became a star eight years later in a contemporary play called "The Fortune Hunter." He then played in a series of hits, among them "Peter Ibbetson," at the Shubert in 1917. But he played Shakespeare only once, in New York in 1922, in Boston at the Opera House for one week beginning December 24, 1923, and in London for a few weeks, and then he set the pattern for so many who would follow: he went away to Hollywood. When he tried to come back,

many years later, touring in a sad little play called "My Dear Children," he was no more than a caricature of John Barrymore.

Brando began acting in New York as a young man with obviously abundant talent and strong personality. He appeared with Katharine Cornell as Marchbanks in "Candida" and was immediately noticed.

In 1946, he made his first Boston appearance and was fired the first night. In a play called "Eagle Rampant," adapted from the French of

*The young and beautiful Ethel Barrymore in "Captain Jinks of the Horse Marines," in which she became a star. Offstage, she won the hearts of all Bostonians and such Londoners as Winston Churchill, who proposed. What if Ethel had said yes?*

*Ethel Barrymore, one of the greatest American stars of the twentieth century.*

Jean Cocteau, he acted in support of Tallulah Bankhead at the Plymouth Theater. He had a death scene in which he was required to die on a platform three or four steps up from the stage; he chose to make it a little bigger than Tallulah Bankhead believed necessary. Instead of simply dying, he wrapped himself in a portiere and rolled all the way down the stairs. Tallulah said "You may say you have resigned, but please go away!" He went away, and nobody paid much attention. He returned to Boston a year later as Stanley Kowalski in "A

Streetcar Named Desire," opposite Jessica Tandy at the Wilbur Theater, and became a superstar overnight. Then he, too, went to Hollywood, and although he made a strange tour of the summer theaters in a muddled version of Shaw's "Arms and the Man" (which played a moviehouse in nearby Framingham), has stayed there ever since.

I do not suggest that his films, or some of those of Barrymore, are inferior. On the contrary, the best of those that I have seen and his performances in them, are extraordinary. But Brando—like Spencer Tracy and Gregory Peck, and Kirk Douglas, and so many more—by failing to accept the old tradition, the obligation to test themselves in the greatest acting roles, have denied American

*E. H. Sothern. An American star in the classical tradition, he often appeared as co-star with Julia Marlowe.*

*Walter Hampden, a Harvard man who became a distinguished classical actor. His most popular role was Cyrano de Bergerac.*

theatergoers the right to see them at the peak of their power, and to see the classics of the drama in great American performances. Think of what it would have been like to watch the young Gregory Peck as Romeo! Or Tracy as Macbeth or Lear. Or Brando in just about anything that Edwin Booth or Edwin Forrest ever played.

They couldn't break away from all those million-dollar movies? The British do. Olivier does. So do Gielgud and Richardson and Alec Guinness and Peter O'Toole and Richard Burton and the unpredictable Nicol Williamson. A few years back Peter O'Toole made a movie about Lawrence of Arabia, for which he had his hair dyed blond and

in which he portrayed the great English hero. When that film was completed, he went back to London, washed the dye out of his hair, and for something like $200 a week played Shylock in "The Merchant of Venice" at the Old Vic. If one of our American stars had made such a film, he would have returned to this country, keeping that lovely blond gilt in his hair, gone to Palm Springs, and waited by his swimming pool for one that would probably be called "Lawrence of Afghanistan." The theater? Shakespeare? Too dangerous, old boy. Those New York critics, you know!

*Ethel Barrymore as the schoolteacher, Miss Moffat, in Emlyn Williams' "The Corn Is Green," her last role in Boston (1942).*

# CHAPTER VI
## TO CATCH THE CONSCIENCE OF THE KING

The "Metamora" that Edwin Forrest made famous is typical of one kind of play that was popular in Boston and elsewhere in the nineteenth century, and which can fairly be called "heroic melodrama." Melodrama is like tragedy in that it deals with events of solemn consequence; but it tends to focus on danger rather than disaster, and its characters are types, or stereotypes, rather than individuals. Lear is a magnificent human being, Chief Metamora a theatrical stereotype. There are many kinds of melodrama, including, for example, mystery melodramas, like "Sherlock Holmes," which William Gillette brought to Boston time and again, and in our time "Sleuth," which we imported from England in 1976. Heroic melodrama is concerned not with solving the problems of "who done it," but with exhibiting heroes larger than life. Heroic melodrama is not common today in our theater, which tends to favor nonheroes, but Hollywood still gives us a few. There is a close likeness between "The Gladiator," which was also a favorite of Edwin Forrest's, comparable in popularity in Boston and elsewhere to his "Metamora," and the Kirk Douglas film "Spartacus." Both are based on the same legend; both were produced in the same basic style. "The Count of Monte Cristo," for which there is still an audience, is another in this genre. So is "Ben-Hur," which opened the Colonial Theater in 1900.

Along with heroic plays, Bostonians of the nineteenth century learned to admire sentimental melodrama, which, as in the cases of "The Old Homestead" and the preceding "Joshua Whitcomb" and "Rip Van Winkle," deals with characters who are not heroic but kindly, who are closer to sinful human nature, and are not threatened by grave danger; also, the great moral melodramas, one of which was "The Drunkard, or, the Fallen Saved," the first long-run play at the Boston Museum. It opened February 25, 1844, for the first time, was repeated next year for a total of one hundred performances, and returned again and again. Another, of course, was "Uncle Tom's Cabin," which was presented at the Boston Theater ten times in the period between 1857 and 1897—though never for a long run to match those of "The Old Homestead"—and was shown, too, at the Boston Museum in various versions. At one performance, Harriet Beecher Stowe, visiting the theater for what seems to have been the first time, reportedly walked out because of comedy that had been interpolated and that she considered offensive.

Romantic melodrama, another variety, centers on the hazards faced by noble young men and innocent young ladies in love, developed from Shakespeare's "Romeo and Juliet" and "Twelfth Night" and, like ancient melodrama, nearly always associated with music. It began to take hold of our Boston public with the first production here in 1908 of the Viennese operetta "The Merry Widow," and in the concurrent development of musical comedy, which is similar to operetta yet significantly different. Operetta deals with events and characters remote from American life: with princes, for example, who fall in love with waitresses and who will always keep them deep in their hearts, dear. Musical comedy usually finds rich and handsome young fellows, too, but the scene is contemporary America. And where the basic operetta of Vienna set its love sings to waltz tunes, American musical comedy began to adopt in the first ten years of the twentieth century our own varieties of song and dance, from the one-step to the turkey trot to the Charleston and the jitterbug.

Nov. 8, 1920

# BOSTON THEATRE,
## FEDERAL STREET.

STAGE MANAGER . . . . MR. JOHN G. GILBERT.

# THANKSGIVING NIGHT!

*NINTH NIGHT OF*

# MR. FORREST

PRICES—Parquet Seats, and Private and Proscenium Box tickets, $1; Boxes, 50 cents; Pit, 25 cents; Gallery 12½ cents. No money can be taken at the Doors.
DOORS OPEN at 6 1-4 o'clock; Curtain will be raised at 1-4 before 7 precisely.

ENTRANCES—To Boxes, also Boxes G, H, I, J, K, L, M, N, O, P, Q, R—on Federal street. To Private Boxes A, B, C, D, E, F, and to Chairs in Parquet, on Franklin street. To Pit and Gallery, in alley on Federal street.

## Thursday Evening, Nov. 26, 1846

*BY REQUEST, THE INDIAN TRAGEDY OF*

# METAMORA!

—OR THE—

## *Last of the Wampanoags.*

### INDIANS.

| | | | |
|---|---|---|---|
| METAMORA | (his original character) | | MR. FORREST |
| Kaushine | Mr. S. D. Johnson | Nahmeokee | Mrs. Bland |
| Otah | Stephens | Child | Mast. Johnson |
| Anawandah | Bond | Indian Warriors. | |

### COLONISTS.

| | | | |
|---|---|---|---|
| Mordaunt, Exile and Regicide, | Mr. Gilbert | Wolfe, follower of Lord Fitz } | Mr. Benson |
| Lord Fitz Arnold | W. Germon | Arnold | |
| Sir Arthur Vaughan | Brydges | Goodenough, a Puritan Soldier, | Parsons |
| Errington, Chief of the Council, | Whiting | Officer | Parker |
| Walter | Bland | Soldiers of the Colony, Peasants, &c. | |
| Capt. Church, Leader of the } Puritan Army | H. Russell | Oceana, Daughter of Mordaunt, | Mrs. H. Cramer |
| Tramp | Adams | | |

To conclude with the laughable Farce, by Buckstone, entitled the

# Irish Lion!

| | | | |
|---|---|---|---|
| Tim Moore | Mr Brougham | Mr Slim | Mr Parsons |
| Mr Squabbs | Brydges | Mr Yawkins | King |
| Mr Puffy | Whiting | | |
| Capt. Dixon | Stephens | Mrs Cerulia Fitzgig | Mrs W. H. Smith |
| Wadd | Benson | Mrs Crummy | Mrs Mueller |
| Ginger | S. D. Johnson | Miss Echo | Miss Wagstaff |
| John Long | Adams | Miss Titter | Miss Boquet |
| Mr Mackenzie | W. Germon | Miss Jenks | Miss Mack |
| Mr Shindy | Parker | Mrs Jones | Mrs Deluce |

☞FRIDAY—Mr. FORREST will appear. In Rehearsal, the celebrated Tragedy of the GLADIATOR, with New Scenery and Dresses, in which Mr Forrest will appear.

EASTBURN'S PRESS—18 STATE STREET.

From 1900 until "Lady in the Dark" in 1941, musical comedy concerned itself with very young men and women in love. Then Gertrude Lawrence, Mary Martin, Ethel Merman, and Ezio Pinza began to add years, and middle-aged lovers became attractive to an audience that by the time of "Annie, Get Your Gun" and "South Pacific" had become, much to its own surprise, middle-aged too.

In Europe at the end of the nineteenth century, new playwrights began to turn the theater away from melodrama to plays that would truthfully depict contemporary life as they saw it. Melodrama reflected and confirmed the moral, social, and political convictions of its time. Heroes and heroines were upright, villains were the sort of people— and, by the way, they were always men—whom society deplored. The new drama of Europe, beginning with the revolutionary social plays of Henrik Ibsen, such as "A Doll's House" in 1879, and most of those of George Bernard Shaw, broke away from heroes to present contemporary middle-class men and women, not endorsing but challenging the ideas of society.

In 1887 in Paris, Andre Antoine opened one of the first of the new "little theaters," the Théâtre Libre, to make possible the production of these radical new dramas of Ibsen and the Swedish giant, Strindberg, some of which horrified and appalled critics and audiences alike, because instead of endorsing the accepted wisdom of their day they ridiculed or challenged it.

In Boston, with the endorsement of William Dean Howells, a group of young people got together in 1891 and in old Chickering Hall put on a play called "Margaret Fleming," which they hoped would be the first of several in the repertory of what might become an American *théâtre libre*. By our present-day standards, "Margaret Fleming" is not a shocker. But in its day it was a groundbreaker, not so much because the playwright,

opposite: *Program for Edwin Forrest's greatest success, "Metamora," at the Boston Theater in 1846. He was supported by the resident stock company.*

James A. Herne, defied the conventions of society as because he dared violate those of our playgoers, who didn't care to see on the stage people like themselves facing ugly moral problems such as adultery and physical hazards too: the woman of the title is going blind from glaucoma.

A little later, a whole American school of playwrights, among them Eugene O'Neill, would begin to follow the lead of the Europeans, breaking with precedent. O'Neill was articulate about why he began to write as he did of the grief and desperation of modern men and women. For one thing, he said, his new realistic dramas, "Desire Under the Elms," for example, and "Strange Interlude," were not merely a reflection of his personal views about life; they were written deliberately in reaction against the popular plays in which his father had appeared, especially "The Count of Monte Cristo," which he knew not only as the son of James O'Neill but as an actor who had appeared in the old chestnut.

O'Neill was followed by others in the twenties, thirties, and forties. They were, of course, motivated by social, political, and moral convictions, but they shared his belief that the old melodramas of the nineteenth and early twentieth centuries, the "Monte Cristos" and the "Ben-Hurs" and the "Metamoras," were false and fraudulent. They aimed for truth to life in their own time, using the new forms of theatrical "realism" and "naturalism." In Boston, this brought many of them into conflict with public opinion, and with the law.

There were other reasons why we got our first city censor in 1904, but this was one. The new Americans, following Ibsen and Strindberg, and to a certain extent Shaw, were putting the audience itself on the stage in circumstances our playgoers didn't like, in the language of the sitting room and sometimes that of the street, and not merely disturbing their convictions but offending their sensibilities. The first plays of Henrik Ibsen were denounced in London and New York as shocking, even monstrous. Boston, with its old strains of Puritanism and its new moral rigidity preached by religious leaders the Puritans would have hated, was particularly hostile.

Before getting down to specifics on this subject, let me go back to the earlier theater of Boston to consider some of the other kinds of dramatic entertainment which our theatergoers admired. There were, for one genre, patriotic plays of various kinds, among them Royall Tyler's "The Contrast," which jeered at those Americans who aped the English; this was presented at the New Exhibition Room in 1793. There was also "The Battle of Bunker Hill," subtitled "The Death of General Warren," which was produced at the Haymarket Theater four years later for the first time in America; it was the work of a Boston editor, John D. Burk.

Farces were popular, most of them brief and broad, presented invariably after serious dramas (including the classics), following a tradition established in Shakespeare's time. These seem to have been assembled rather than written, but were enjoyed by pretty nearly everyone and gave some local actors a large part of their reputation: William Warren, for example, who was a member of the Boston Museum stock company for thirty years and an excellent actor, seems to have been particularly admired for the slapstick tricks he invented for these afterpieces.

These short comedies began to fall into disfavor towards the end of the nineteenth century. In the meantime, a Bostonian named Charles H. Hoyt, who had been a reporter on the Boston *Post*, started writing farce comedies that were more fully developed, long enough to run for an entire evening. Hoyt is important in other ways—he was one of the first playwrights to test his plays in what we have learned to call tryouts—but he is of special concern because his full-length farces anticipated those of later dramatists like George S. Kaufman, Moss Hart and Neil Simon. One of these, "A Trip to Chinatown," opened at the Boston Theater on February 9, 1891, for two good weeks, then went on to New York for 657 performances.

*"Uncle Tom's Cabin" played across the country for more than half a century. This playbill is from one of the first performances in Boston.*

Opera, another conventional form that pleased Bostonians almost from the first, was presented down through the years in the major playhouses in lieu of plays or other entertainment many, many times, until the building in 1909 of the Boston Opera House. On September 2, 1829, "The Barber of Seville" was produced at the old theater on Federal Street, followed by Rossini's "Tancredi." The same year, the competing Tremont Theater presented "The Barber" too, along with "The Beggar's Opera," both sung by members of the Italian Opera Company, which starred a Madame Feron, French-born but trained in Italy.

Productions of grand opera were common at the Tremont as long as it lasted. In its great days in the middle of the nineteenth century the Howard Athenaeum often played opera, generally very successfully, and the second Boston Theater on Washington Street was considered an opera house; for three years, beginning in 1860, its name was changed to Boston Academy of Music.

At the Boston, major singing stars in operas alternated with great and little acting stars in classics on the one hand and popular melodramas on the other, and, from time to time, with variety shows or performances by dancers, or minstrel shows. Beginning April 1, 1901, the Metropolitan Opera Company played the Boston Theater with such stars as Schumann-Heink, Lillian Nordica, and Nellie Melba, under the direction of Walter Damrosch, for one. They followed Denman Thompson in "The Old Homestead," two melodramas ("The Still Alarm" and "A Runaway Girl"), and a minstrel show troupe. When they closed their season, audiences at the Boston got a chance to see, beginning April 15, Sarah Bernhardt and Constantin Coquelin,

*The first production at the Colonial Theater was the spectacular "Ben-Hur," which opened the playhouse in 1900. In this playbill, note that the two principal roles were played by William Farnum and W. S. Hart; both later became silent movie stars, and for a long time William S. Hart rode the range in Hollywood's first Westerns.*

# Colonial Theatre

RICH, HARRIS & CHARLES FROHMAN, — — — — Lessees and Managers.
ISAAC B. RICH, — — — — — — — — — Resident Manager.

☞ *Each lady who during the performance removes her hat, aigrette, or any ornament for the hair—which obstructs the view of anyone in the audience—shows a graceful consideration for the pleasure of others.*

**WEEK OF DECEMBER 31, 1900.**

Curtain will rise Evenings at 7.45.          Wednesday and Saturday Matinees at 2.

## KLAW & ERLANGER'S

### Production of GEN. LEW WALLACE'S

# BEN-HUR

Under the direction of JOSEPH BROOKS. Arranged for the stage by WM. YOUNG. Vocal and Instrumental Music composed for the production by EDGAR STILLMAN KELLEY. Entire production under stage direction of Ben Teal.

### CHARACTERS IN THE PRELUDE:

| | |
|---|---|
| Balthazar, the Egyptian | Francis Kingdon |
| Gaspar, the Greek | F. S. Thorpe |
| Melchior, the Hindoo | Chas. J. Wilson |

### CHARACTERS IN THE DRAMA:

| | |
|---|---|
| Ben-Hur, Judah, son of Ithamar | William Farnum |
| Messala | W. S. Hart |
| Simonides | Emmett Corrigan |
| Arrius, the Tribune | Robert Elliot |
| Balthazar | Francis Kingdon |
| Ilderim | Henry Weaver, Jr. |
| Malluch | John F. Cook |
| Hortator | Chas. J. Wilson |
| Metellus | Franclyn Roberts |
| Drusus | W. J. Kelly |
| Cecilius | Henry T. Devere |
| Sanballat | Robert Mansfield |
| Khaled | Charles Craig |
| Centurion | H. DeForest |
| Officer of the Galley | J. Stuart Clark |
| Esther | Nellie Thorne |
| Iras | Adele Block |
| Mother of Hur | Mabel Burt |
| Tirzah | Adeline Adler |
| Amrah | Mary Shaw |

### SYNOPSIS OF SCENES.

Prelude—Curtain symbolic of Rome and Jerusalem (Albert)—The Desert (Albert)—Meeting of the Three Wise Men.

"* * In the morning arise, and go and meet them. And when ye have all come to the holy city, Jerusalem, ask of the people, ' Where is He that is born King of the Jews?—for we have seen His Star in the East, and are sent to worship Him.' * * *

"Suddenly in the air before them, not further up than a low hilltop, flared a lambent flame. As they looked at it the apparition contracted into a focus of dazzling lustre. * * And they shouted as with one voice, ' The Star! The Star!' "—Ben-Hur, Book I, Chap. 5.

ACT I—Scene 1—Housetop of the Palace of Hur, Jerusalem (Albert).—"The Power of Rome."

ACT II—Scene 1—Interior of Cabin of the Roman Galley "Astrea" (Albert),—The Galley Slave. Scene 2—The Open Sea (Albert).—The Rescue.

ACT III—Scene 1—Apartment in the house of Simonides, in Antioch (Gros).—The Wise Servant and His Daughter. Scene 2—The Grove of Daphne—Temple of Apollo (Gros).

"The Grove of Daphne! Nobody can describe it—only beware! It was begun by Apollo, and completed by him. He prefers it to Olympus. People go there for one look—just one—and never come away. They have a saying which tells it all: ' Better be a worm and feed on the mulberries of Daphne, than a king's guest.' "—Ben-Hur, Book IV, Chap. 2.—The Masque of Eros.

Scene 3—The Fountain of Castalia (Gros).—The Revels of Daphne.—In the Spider's Web.

ACT IV—Scene 1—The Dowar in the Orchard of Palms (Gros).—Preparing for the Race. Scene 2—By the Lake (Gros).—The Arts of Cleopatra.

ACT V—Scene 1—Exterior and Great Gateway of Circus, Antioch (Albert).—Making the Wagers. Scene 2—The Arena (Albert).—The Race.

ACT VI—Scene 1—Apartment in the Palace of Hur, Jerusalem (Albert).—Tidings of the Lost Ones. Scene 2—The Vale of Hinnom (Albert).—The Vision. Scene 3—Mount Olivet (Albert).—The Miracle.

"Now, however, about the commencement of the fourth hour, a great crowd appeared over the crest of Olivet; and as it defiled down the road, thousands in number, the watchers noticed with wonder that every one in it carried a palm-branch, freshly cut."—Ben-Hur, Book VIII, Chap. 4.

—Grand Chorus: " Hosanna! Hosanna! Hosanna in the Highest!"

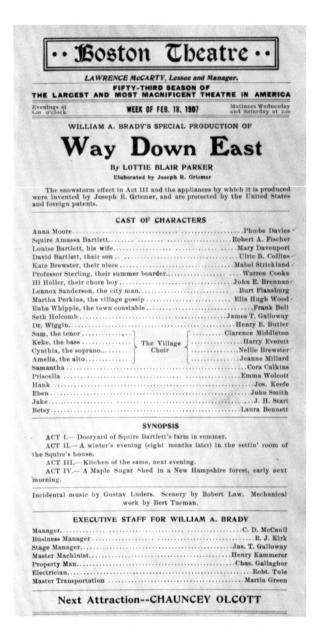

*One of the favorite melodramas of the early 20th century, "Way Down East," which became a famous silent movie, played the Boston Theater in 1907. The author, Lottie Blair Parker, was a former member of the stock company at the same theater.*

*James O'Neill, father of Eugene, shown as he looked offstage at the height of his career. On the opposite page is the program for one of his many Boston appearances in "The Count of Monte Cristo."*

in among other plays, "Cyrano de Bergerac." All these in the one theater in the space of three months.

Comic opera became a favorite form of Bostonians with the first production in America of "H.M.S. Pinafore" at the Boston Museum November 25, 1878. Our love affair with Gilbert and Sullivan, beginning then and there, has continued without a break..

Still another form of entertainment that pleased

# THE GLOBE THEATRE PROGRAMME

## Globe Theatre

**Opening of the Fall and Winter Season.**

### MONDAY EV'NG. OCT. 1

The management begs to announce that the Regular Season at this house will be marked by a new and distinguishing policy, made feasible by the peculiar resources of the establishment, and whereby **Legitimate Stars** and **First Class Combinations** are engaged for various periods, alternating with **An Admirable Company**, especially engaged for competent dramatic illustration, forming a pleasing contrast of attractions. **Appropriate Appointments** and **New Scenery** will lend effect to the several offerings and proper attention will be given to all stage details.

**FOR THE INITIAL PERFORMANCE**

Mr. Stetson has the honor to present his

### MONTE CRISTO

COMPANY,

Originally organized under his management for

**BOOTH'S THEATRE, NEW YORK.**

THE YOUNG AMERICAN ACTOR,

### Mr. JAS. O'NEILL

AS EDMUND DANTES,

ORIGINALLY PLAYED BY HIM WITH GREAT SUCCESS

and a

**NOTABLE ENSEMBLE OF ARTISTS**

In Dumas' Romantic Play,

### MONTE CRISTO

**THE BRILLIANT CAST**

— EMBRACES —

Messrs. Frederic de Belleville, Geo. C. Boniface, J. W. Shannon, James Taylor, J. V. Melton, Forrest Robinson, B. Carhart, B. Lewis, F. L. Union, J. Swinburne, F. E. Goldthwaite, M. W. Rowley, Miss Eugenie Blair, Miss Minnie Monk, Miss Stella Rees.

**ILLUSTRATED WITH**

### ENTIRE NEW SCENERY

BY

**WM. VOEGTLIN and JOS. CLARE,**

Formerly Artists of Booth's Theatre,

### Grand Realistic Effects

AND CORRECT APPOINTMENTS.

Under the Stage Direction of

Mr. ARTHUR LeCLERCQ.

Matinees Wednesday at 2 Saturday

Sale of Seats now progressing.

---

# GLOBE THEATRE

Mr. JOHN STETSON .................................................. PROPRIETOR and MANAGER

**EXECUTIVE DEPARTMENT.**

| | |
|---|---|
| Assistant Manager ............ Mr. Chas. Burnham | Treasurer ............ Mr. Martin Drake |
| Secretary ............ Mr. W. H. Bingham | Musical Director ............ Mr. J. C. Mullaly |
| Stage Director ............ Mr. J. P. Cooke | Gas Engineer ............ Mr. Wm. Dixon |
| Master Machinist ............ Mr. J. Prior | Properties ............ Mr. Chas. Henry |

### MONDAY, OCTOBER 1st, 1883,
### OPENING OF THE REGULAR SEASON

### MR. JOHN STETSON'S
# MONTE CRISTO
COMPANY,

ORIGINALLY ORGANIZED UNDER HIS MANAGEMENT FOR BOOTH'S THEATRE, NEW YORK.

The Popular Young Actor,

## MR. JAMES O'NEILL

AS EDMUND DANTES,

In Dumas' Great Play,

# MONTE CRISTO

With the following Brilliant Star Cast:

| | |
|---|---|
| **EDMUND DANTES and COUNT de MONTE CRISTO** | **Mr. JAMES O'NEILL** |
| NORTIER | Mr. FREDERIC DE BELLEVILLE |
| ALBERT de MORCERF | Mr. FORREST ROBINSON |
| VILLEFORT | Mr. GEO. C. BONIFACE |
| FERNANDE | Mr. J. V. MELTON |
| DANGLARS | Mr. JAMES TAYLOR |
| CADEROUSSE | Mr. J. W. SHANNON |
| ABBE FARIA | Mr. HORACE LEWIS |
| M. MOREL | Mr. J. L. CARHART |
| OLD DANTES | Mr. J. SWINBURNE |
| PENLLON | Mr. DUNN |
| 1st POLICE AGENT | Mr. A. WOOD |
| LeMarq. DeARAMBURO | Mr. FARRAR |
| M. MASSINET | Mr. KNIGHTS |
| M. DANGUERA | Mr. HOLMAN |
| GERBAIN | Mr. F. L. UNION |
| GOVERNOR OF PRISON | Mr. PELHAM |
| 2d GAOLER | Mr. RAWLEY |
| MAN | Mr. ALLEN |
| BRIGADIER | Mr. F. E. GOLTHWAITE |
| 2d POLICE AGENT | Mr. W. WILLIAMS |
| SIGNOR CABRILLIO | Mr. JONES |
| SIG. BATTIOZI | Mr. C. A. RHODES |
| M. BLANC JOUR | Mr. EVERLAN |
| COM. OF POLICE | Mr. CLARK |
| 1st GAOLER | Mr. G. MUELLER |
| SENTINEL | Mr. DAVERINE |
| SERVANT | Mr. B. SLATER |
| FISHERMAN | Mr. J. WHITE |
| MERCEDES | Miss EUGENIE BLAIR |
| CARCONTI | Miss MINNIE MONK |
| MLLE DANGLARS | Miss STELLA REES |
| MAD. LA MARQUISE D'ARAMBURO | Miss EMMA SMITH |
| M'LLE De BEAUPLAN | Miss CARRIE NOYES |
| MLLE De LISLE | Miss ETTA DIXON |
| M'LLE De COURCEY | Miss SCOTT |
| FISHERWOMAN | Miss FLORINA |

**ENTIRE NEW SCENERY** .................. by WM. VOEGTLIN and JOSEPH CLARE

Grand Realistic Effects and Perfect Appointments.

### ACTION OF THE PLAY.

**ACT ONE.**
The Port of Marseilles.
Scene 2.—Villefort's Cabinet. Scene 3.—The Reserve Inn. Edmund Dantes' Wedding Day. The Fete Interrupted. Arrest of Edmund Dantes. (A lapse of eighteen years between the 1st and 2d Acts.)

**The Conspiracy.**

**ACT THREE.**
The Roadside Inn. The First Blow of Vengeance. ONE.

**ACT TWO.**
The Prison of the Chateau D'If. The Treasure of Monte Cristo. Escape of Edmund Dantes.

**THE WORLD IS MINE.**

**ACT FOUR.**
Grand Fete in the Illuminated Gardens of Hotel de Morcerf. The Recognition. The quarrel. The Challenge. "I will kill you." "You will not." "Why?" "He is your son."

**ACT FIVE.**
The Forest of Fontainebleau. The Revenge of Monte Cristo. Suicide of Fernande. TWO. The Duel. Death of Danglars. THREE. Grand Denouement. Paid in Full.

**MATINEES** ............................................ WEDNESDAY (at 2) SATURDAY

--- **POPULAR PRICES** ---

| | |
|---|---|
| General Admission to all parts of the House ............ 50 Cents. | |
| Orchestra Entire and Balcony Circle (two rows) ............ $1.00 | |
| Orchestra Circle ............ .75 | Proscenium Boxes ............ $6, $8 and $10.00 |
| Balcony ............ .75 | Balcony Boxes (5, 6 and 8 Chairs) ............ $5, $6 and $8.00 |
| Second Balcony ............ .50 | Gallery ............ 25 Cents |

Until further notice, doors open at 1.30 and 7.30 ............ Performance commences at 2 and 8

Patrons will please report to the proprietor any inattention on the part of the attaches of this theatre.

The Chickering Piano only used in this Theatre. Warerooms, 156 Tremont.

The celebrated New England Organ Co.'s Cabinet Organs used in this Theatre.

Parties having secured seats will find it to their advantage to enter by the Essex Street entrance.

OPERA GLASSES TO LET IN THE LADIES' CLOAK ROOM. CARRIAGES may be called at the Essex or Washington St. entrance

SMOKING ROOM located over the Washington Street entrance; enter head of stairway leading to the Balcony.

many people here and elsewhere in the United States for nearly a hundred years, until it began to be taken over by radio and then television, was called in the beginning "variety" and a little later "vaudeville." Variety has its roots in the European past, when itinerant fiddlers and dancers first appeared on village greens and in taverns. It was presented here in Colonial times when the Puritan fathers weren't watching, and in the early years of the republic began to be seen more frequently. Along with the moral lectures at the New Exhibition Room, there were programs consisting of a variety of entertainers doing pretty much the same kind of thing a variety of entertainers used to do on the *Ed Sullivan Show:* singing, dancing, tricks and treats.

The Howard Athenaeum was one of the first major playhouses of the nineteenth century to present variety shows, and when it began to lose standing in the competition with the Boston Museum and the second Boston Theater, it relied more and more on these, adding burlesque shows, which until the 1920s were innocent entertainments that parodied serious drama in somewhat the same way that Tom Stoppard's "Travesties" parodies "The Importance of Being Earnest."

Variety tended to be crude in those days. B. F. Keith transformed it into "vaudeville" and made it a great national institution a little later. In the meantime, other showmen had transformed burlesque into something much less amusing by debasing the humor for the delectation of people of little wit, and then introducing strippers for the benefit of curious teenagers and old gentlemen in whom the fires of life had dimmed and needed to be rekindled or at least fanned into a mild glow of warmth.

Keith began with a variety show in his "museum" on Washington Street and in 1894 erected next door B. F. Keith's Theater, the first showcase of the kind built in the style of the major playhouses. Keith's Theater had an orchestra, a bill of eight acts of vaudeville scrupulously policed (a performer who said "hell" or "damn" could be fired), and a reserved seat policy, with two shows a day.

Burlesque in its original form had been popular

---

# HOLLIS ST. THEATRE

### BOSTON

*Engagement of two weeks only*

## May 21 to June 2, 1928

## EVA LeGALLIENNE and the New York Civic Repertory Theatre

*Plays to be presented:*

**"THE GOOD HOPE"**
*By* HEIJERMANS

| | |
|---|---|
| Monday Night ......May 21 | ☐ |
| Wednesday Matinee ..May 23 | ☑ |
| Friday Night .......May 25 | ☑ |
| Saturday Night ......May 26 | ☑ |
| Tuesday Night ......May 29 | ☐ |
| Friday Night .......June 1 | ☐ |

**"HEDDA GABLER"**
*By* IBSEN

| | |
|---|---|
| Tuesday Night ......May 22 | ☐ |
| Wednesday Night ....May 23 | ☐ |
| Saturday Matinee ....May 26 | ☐ |
| Wednesday Matinee ..May 30 | ☑ |
| Thursday Night .....May 31 | ☐ |
| Saturday Night ......June 2 | ☐ |

**"LA LOCANDIERA"**
*By* GOLDONI

| | |
|---|---|
| Thursday Night .....May 24 | ☐ |
| Saturday Matinee ....June 2 | ☑ |

**"THE CRADLE SONG"**
*By* SIERRA

| | |
|---|---|
| Monday Night ......May 28 | ☐ |
| Wednesday Night ....May 30 | ☐ |
| Friday Matinee ........June 1 | ☐ |

### PRICES (INCLUDING TAX)

| *All Evenings and Saturday Matinees* | *Wednesday Matinees only* |
|---|---|
| Orchestra .................$2.75 | Orchestra .................$1.65 |
| 1st Balcony ...$2.20, $1.65, $1.10 | 1st Balcony ........$1.65, $1.10 |
| 2nd Balcony .............. .50 | 2nd Balcony .............. .50 |

## ORDER BLANK

Enclosed is {Check / Money Order} for $............

in payment for...................Tickets at $.....................
each for the performances indicated above.

*Name* ...............................................................

*Address* .............................................................
Make checks payable to Hollis Street Theatre. Please mail this blank in the enclosed addressed envelope. Orders will be filled in sequence of their receipt.

*Eva Le Gallienne's New York Civic Repertory Theater played the Hollis Street Theater in May, 1928, with a typical program of four plays.*

opposite: *One of the first "musical comedies" to play Boston, "Peggy from Paris" starred William Hodge at the Tremont Theater during the week of May 25, 1903. The humorist George Ade was the author.*

HENRY W. SAVAGE PRESENTS GEORGE ADE'S *New*

# PEGGY FROM PARIS

### Music by WILLIAM LORAINE

## A MUSICAL COMEDY IN A PROLOGUE AND TWO ACTS

### THE CAST:
#### THE PROLOGUE — In Hickory Crick.

Captain Alonzo Plummer, the village dignitary................Wm. T. Hodge
Hon. Jabez Flanders, the village orator..................Goodwal Dickerman
Walt Quackenbush, the village joker.........................Dan Baker
Jim Peasley, the village station agent.....................E. H. O'Connor
Lutie Plummer, the village soprano....................Guelma L. Baker
Mrs. Homer Ketcham, the village news bureau..............Eulalie Jensen
Lem Harvey, the village tenor.......................Chas L. Welch
Tessie Higgins, helping in the kitchen................Olivette Haynes
(NOTE — When the curtain rises on Act I, the stage hands are discovered setting the stage for the reception in honor of Mlle. Fleurette Caramelle.)

#### ACTS I AND II—IN BOSTON:

Cicero J. Grampis, a Napoleon of the drama.........Edward J. Connelly
Captain Alonzo Plummer, of Hickory Crick..............Wm. T. Hodge
Montague Fish, a banker with a private ambition.........George Schiller
Alexander Nerveen, collegian.........................John P. Park
Reginald Hickey, a useful boy......................Arthur Deagon
M. Hommard............⎰ Of the Franco-American ⎱............Dan Baker
M. Folies-Bergere.....⎱ League ⎰...........E. H. O'Connor
Dickey Drexel......................................Geo. F. Bennett
Peggy Plummer, known as Mlle. Fleurette Caramelle........Georgia Caine
Lutie Plummer, her half sister....................Guelma L. Baker
Sophie Blotz, Mlle. Caramelle's maid.................Josie Sadler
Mrs. Montague Fish, a wife..........................Alice Hageman
Lily Ann Lynch, the home-grown article................Helen Hale
Mrs. Tuft-Hunter, a social leader.....................Blanch Gilson
Bell Boys, Amateurs, Collegians, Autograph Girls, Stage Hands, Chappies, Society Leaders, Clubmen, etc., by a large and willing chorus.

#### ACT II—Scene 1.
Bell Boys — Misses Rae, Olivette, Marik, Misses Dalghren and Norman.
Chappies — Messrs. Davis, Welch, Benham, Moore, Bennett, Hollenbeck, Wilson and Randall.
Autograph Girls— Misses Gardner, Hall, Hardren, Willard, Gorman, Lee and Harlow.
#### Scene II — The Reception.
Society Leaders — Misses Reed, Gilson, Cushing, Daniell, York and Mabel Fredericks, Frizzelle, Williamson, Jensen and Olga Fredericks, Arnold, Anderson, Gorman, Mack, Lilja, Willard, Gardner, Hart, Lee, Hardren, Hall, Henderson, Harlow, James and Wilson.
Cupids — Misses Olivette, Rae, Marik, Misses Dalghren and Norman.
Clubmen — Messrs. Davis, Welch, Benham, Chadwick, Moore.
Flunkies — Messrs. Randall, DeMers, Bosher and Hollenbeck.

PROLOGUE — Main parlor of the Commercial Hotel, Hickory Crick, Ill. The Old Times Party.
ACT I — The stage of the Paragon Theatre, Boston. The getting together of the Plummers, two minutes between prologue and Act I.
ACT II—Scene 1. Reception room of Peggy's apartments, Hotel Touraine. The new man-servant. Scene 2—Mrs. Tuft-Hunter's private Casino.

#### MUSICAL SYNOPSIS.
##### Scene I
Overture.
1. Opening Chorus—" Happy, Happy Illinois.
2. "Highfalutin Music."
3. " Old Fashioned Songs."
4. "The Limited Train."
##### Scene II.
5. Opening Chorus—" We are the Principals."

##### ACT I.
6. "Football Song." Music by R. P. Dunlap.
7. " Art."
8. " Emmaleen."
9. " The Girl Who Comes In from the West."
10. " Welcome."
11. "Gay Fleurette."
12. Finale.

##### ACT II.
13. " When He's Not Near."
14. "Chappies' Song."
15. Autograph Girls' Song.
16. "Henny."
17. Between Scenes I and II Lunita Intermezzo.
18. Ensemble—" Here's Happy Days to You."
19. "Tell-Tale Eyes," by W. C. Powell.
20. "Lil, I Like You."
21. " I Left my Heart in Dixie."
22. Finale.
Musical numbers published by M. Witmark & Son. For sale in foyer.

The dancing arranged by Joseph C. Smith. Costumes designed by Will R. Barnes, executed by Fritz Schoultz & Co., Mme. Freisinger and E. A. Armstrong.
Scenery by Mr. Walter C. Burridge. Mechanical effects by Thomas F. Tipping. Electrical effects by Samuel Budd. Properties by Wm. Young. Wigs by J. Ibe. Shoes by Alston & Co. Flowers by Boganski.

#### EXECUTIVE STAFF FOR MR HENRY W. SAVAGE.
George A. Kingsbury............General Manager
Madison Corey.................Acting Manager
Mason Peters..................Business Manager
William M. Roddy.............Advertising Agent
Frank Todd....................Stage Director
E. H. O'Connor ...............Stage Manager
P. T. Johnston ..............Master Mechanic
Edward Gateley ...............Electrician
Wm. J. Carter ...........Master Properties
Walter Burridge ..............Scenic Artist
Samuel Chadwick ......Assistant Stage Manager
Mrs. Olive Corbett .........Wardrobe Mistress

here since early in the nineteenth century, when English humorists began to put on plays that mocked the popular serious dramas. There was one, for instance, in 1842 called "Tap-I-O-Kee," which made fun of "Metamora" and similar melodramas about noble savages. The British, who developed this form to an art, inspired a Bostonian named Edward E. Rice to create American shows of the same kind with original songs and dances and lots of pretty girls. His most celebrated burlesque, "Evangeline," in 1874, was a travesty of Longfellow's "Evangeline" and "Hiawatha." Another one of forty or fifty shows of the kind that he produced over a period of thirty years originated here in a show sponsored by the First Corps of Cadets; called "1492 Up to Date, or Very Near It," it burlesqued the celebrations then being held in honor of Christopher Columbus.

The rowdier forms of burlesque, which became notorious in the Howard, the Gaiety, the Casino, the Park (under the Minsky brothers), and the Globe theaters, started with brief parodies mixed with variety acts. Then, competing with other forms of public entertainment for audiences that didn't understand parody, it began to develop the striptease out of earlier and more timid displays known by such names as "living models." As the strippers came in, wit went out, and eventually so did good taste, and, in the last desperate years, so did any semblance of decency. Comedians, pushed into the background, degenerated to the level of pimps.

Another form of musical show which became a great Boston favorite is revue. The oldest revue in

*overleaf: Program of the Howard Athenaeum which began as a legitimate theater and opera house, then started to play "variety," the ancestor of vaudeville. This program is of a typical bill, with a variety of acts; the second half included a burlesque show called "Hassenbad," a playlet that mocked solemn "Oriental" drama. Later, in the 1920's, this form was corrupted into the bolder kind of burlesque with droopy pants comics and dropping pants ladies.*

VOL. I.     MONDAY, OCTOBER 25th, 1880.     NO. 49.

# HOWARD ATHENÆUM.

**WILLIAM HARRIS,**    .   .   .    **Sole Manager.**
**FRANK WRIGHT,**    -    -    **Stage Manager,**

OVERTURE, Medley from "Mulligan Guard Picnic," latest by D. Braham,
..............................HARRY SAXTON'S ORCHESTRA

Followed by the Laughable Sketch,

## A FUNNY STORY.

Baldy Winfield ....... ..... ... .............Ben Gilfoil
Frank Wright,   DeWitt Cook   James Hearne.

On account of Mr. Kerrigan's severe illness, he will be unable to appear, but his partner,

## DAN McCARTHY,

Will dance some of his electric Irish Reels.

## MR. LARRY TOOLEY,

The ever-welcome Dutch Comique, appearing in some of his peculiar eccentricities and laughable creations.

## DE WITT COOKE,

The King of Clubs.—This gentleman has by years of labor perfected the Manipulation of the Kehoe Clubs.

Those sterling burlesque operatic sketch artists,

## Mr. Fred—HALLEN and HART,—Miss Enid

Who will introduce their original, laughable, tragical, comical, operatical, eccentric, musical comedy,

### Pinafore in Fifteen Minutes.

Tom Twaddle, a universal genius, who, like everybody else, is gone on Pinafore................................... ...... .....Fred Hallen
Sarah Bubles, a girl of the kitchen, with a love for opera.... ..... ....Enid Hart

## JAMES HEARNE,

The Refined Irish Vocalist and Dancer.

First appearance in Boston of the American Four since their return from California,

## AMERICAN 4 AMERICAN

Pettingill, Gale, Daly & Hoey.    The only four that produces original business.

## MISS NELLIE PARKER,

The most fascinating Serio-Comique in existence.

CONTINUED ON SECOND PAGE.

## PROGRAMME.

# ALEX. DAVIS,

**The World's Premier Ventriloquist.** His first appearance in three years, since his triumphant tour through Great Britain, Belgium, Russia and Germany. Undoubtedly the greatest card in America, to-day.

Performance to conclude with Lillie Hall's Burlesque, entitled,

# HASSENBAD;

## IN FIVE SCENES.

HASSENBAD, in love with Medina, who when he has a fit of the blues *has 'em bad,* . . . . . . . . . . . . . . . . . . . . . . . . . . . MISS LILLIE HALL

JEZABEL, Medina's nurse, *jes' a belle*, too you bet . . . . MR. CHAS. FOSTELLE

King Aboolijohn, though *flushed* sometimes with wine, generally *has a jack* full, therefore called a *bully john* . . . . . . . . . . . Mr. Frank Wright

Billy Bowlegs, a jolly tar, a rover of the seas, sometimes half seas over . . . . . . . . . . . . . . . . . . . . . . . . . . . . . . . . . . . . . . . . . . . . . Mr. Ben Gilfoi

Princess Medina, taken from the old song, "Come and Kiss me Dinah," . . . . . . . . . . . . . . . . . . . . . . . . . . . . . . . Miss Annie Boyd

Salaam, who, not being able to repeat the old nursery rhyme "Bah! Bah! Black Sheep," could only *say lamb* . . . . . . Miss Kate Taylor

Hop-light-loo . . . . . . . . . . . . . . . . . . . . . . . . . . . . . . . . . . . . . Mr. Larry Tooley

Guards, Lords, Ladies in waiting, etc.

Grand Evolutions by Twenty Ladies, Clad in Elegant New Armors, manufactured by Bloom, Bowery, N. Y., especially for this attraction.

The elegant Fountain used in the Burlesque, is kindly furnished by the Oakes Manufacturing Co., 111 Washington Street.

### Week Commencing Nov. 1st,

**MINNIE OSCAR GREY,    WM. T. STEPHENS,**

And the Dramatic Dogs,

*ROMEO, ZIP and HERO,*

—— IN ——

# SAVED FROM THE STORM.

### Tuesday, November 2nd,

**ELELCTION DAY, Grand Extra Matinee at 2.**

# MATINEES:

# Wednesdays and Saturdays

## AT 2.

# Evening Performance

## COMMENCES AT 7.45.

# A GOOD RESERVED SEAT FOR 35 CENTS.

## MATINEE PRICES:

## 10cts, 25cts, 35cts, & 50cts.

existence today is the Folies Bergère of Paris, which has been running for more than a century, sustained in the last fifty years by tourists. It set the pattern that the great American entrepreneur Florenz Ziegfeld followed in his "Ziegfeld Follies," which were presented annually from 1907 till 1932, always in Boston before New York.

Operetta is like musical comedy in that both are light-hearted (sometimes light-minded) and both tell a story (usually a love story), and both use music and dance. Revue is similar in purpose—it is meant to be a light entertainment—but it avoids plot: there is no story, no libretto, but instead a series of sketches, songs, and dances, held together only because they are performed by the same cast. Also, where musical comedy and operetta are senti-mental, true revue tends to be satirical, jeering at the follies of the day.

The Folies Bergère made, and still makes, a point of exhibiting girls of various sizes and shapes in costumes of various sizes and shapes. Ziegfeld found and exhibited, as he advertised, "The Most Beautiful Girls in the World," and at times his costumers dropped all their stitches, creating sensa-tions in the earlier years when women on the streets of Boston were considered daring if they showed so much as an ankle under their long skirts. He, however, did it with some taste, and he usually kept his nude ladies still, because it appears that as "living statues" they were artistic, but as moving beauties they were apt to bring down the wrath of the censor. Some of Ziegfeld's contemporaries, as for instance George White, who had his annual "Scandals," and Earl Carroll, whose shows were sometimes called "Vanities," were less skillful and were utterly lacking in either taste or discretion. They were given to crude comedy very much like that of the burlesque shows, and their girls were given not only to posing but also to frolicking on

the stage. In New York, they backed up the wagon for Carroll; here, he was told to dress some of his ladies, or else. He dressed Gracie Worth, for one, which made it difficult for her to take a bath on-stage in his show "Sketch Book," at the Shubert in October 1930.

The revue form dwindled and disappeared in the thirties, a victim, like the stock companies, of the talkies and the radio programs. The sound movies began to take over the audiences; the radio programs took away those rare, gifted, comic authors who could write brief, bright, funny sketches—blackouts—and paid them more. When television replaced the radio hours, the authors went to television. Meantime, the invention of the bikini made most displays of female bodies on the stage redundant.

In 1955 and 1956, Neil Simon wrote revue sketches with his brother, Dan. Four years later, he composed all the blackouts for a revue called "Little Me" which starred Sid Caesar. Then he discovered (and so did such other sketch writers as Abe Burrows and Woody Allen) that ideas for these brief comedies could profitably be expanded into three-act plays or collected, as in "Plaza Suite," into a whole evening's entertainment, or made into movies—or maybe both. Meantime, most of the comedians who played these sketches had preceded him into television or films.

The revue died, but not before some of its practi-tioners or producers had created as much trouble as merriment in Boston, where their violations of good taste, or of the carefully articulated laws and ordinances, had brought down on them the wrath of the officeholder called officially, then and now, chief of the Licensing Division in the mayor's office, but in the newspapers and in the theater, the city censor.

# CHAPTER VII
## ERA OF THE BIG BANS

Censorship is a difficult and sensitive subject in any city because it involves a curtailment of the right of free speech and free choice, and because its rules, regulations, and practices are sometimes the result of strong religious convictions, customs, or sanctions. In Boston, the practices of our city officials have been bitterly criticized, sometimes ridiculed, because down through the years since 1904 they have sometimes banned plays of established merit, altered others in the text or in production, and because these censorial actions have rarely been duplicated elsewhere. We are thought of as unique, an American city which forbids or mutilates by censorship what is accepted as true or beautiful, or at least harmless, in the rest of the United States. The phrase "banned in Boston" is considered funny now, but over the years it has raised tempers and stirred wrath among our own citizens and outlanders, too.

Despite the press, we never have had here any official with the title "city censor," or with the legal power to restrain theater production that the Lord Chamberlain of London had for so long. The Lord Chamberlain was empowered to prevent the presentation of any play he considered offensive, for any one of a number of reasons. The men who did the banning in Boston down through the years were representatives of the mayor, entitled under the law to do no more than keep an eye on the stage and screen; their official title was "chief of the city's Licensing Division." The authority to suppress, or alter, or challenge the morality of productions belonged to the mayor until 1915, and after that to a committee of three. Technically, the so-called censor was no more than a messenger; actually, in the time of John M. Casey and some of his successors, the office was used more than once to coerce producers. And where the Lord Chamberlain did his censoring by reading manuscripts and approving or rejecting them before productions got under way, our men took action sometimes only after producers had invested a good deal of money and had their shows on the stage.

When John Casey became in effect, if not in name, city censor, some plays were financed by the men who owned the theaters; others were underwritten independently. If the producers of the independent plays refused to accept the orders of the city censor, Casey might choose to vent his displeasure not on them but on the theater owners, and might conceivably keep their playhouses dark for a week, or two, or three. So the theater owners were willing and eager to accept his "suggestions," even when these were whimsical. In the mayoral years of James M. Curley, his censor succeeded in inserting into all contracts between producers and local theater owners a rider, a list of prohibitions, things not to be done on a Boston stage. Violation could mean abrogation of the contract and closing of the theater. Not until 1965, when the Civil Liberties Union won a legal battle to remove that rider, were those restrictions dropped.

The rigidity of Boston theatrical censorship is usually dismissed with indignation as a result of the vagaries of Boston's unusual political system, and it is true that all those who have been identified as city censors have been political appointees, from John M. Casey to Richard J. Sinnott. But more is involved than politics. The Boston way of altering, inhibiting, and occasionally banning shows was rooted in old traditions and attitudes and embodied in laws that originated with the Massachusetts legislature. When the Watch and Ward Society was

formed and began to ban books in a way in which they had never been banned in any other city, it was not Boston politicians, but a combination of Baptist and Methodist clergymen with the most respected booksellers and the most respected newspapers of the city, that screened all books, kept what they considered offensive off the shelves, and saw to it that those books were not reviewed.

The Puritans were long gone when John M. Casey took office, but the puritanical strain was strong in the city and some of its crotchets, especially its insistence on keeping ladies covered from head to foot and keeping men from uttering profane words, had been reinforced by the Victorians. By that time, more than one third of the people of Boston were of Irish extraction, Roman Catholic by religion, and their clergy were more puritancial than Cotton Mather and far more stern and rigid in matters of sexual behavior than Catholics of Italian, German, Polish, or French origin.

*Patrick A. Collins, Mayor of Boston 1902-1905.*

At the end of his career in 1932, John Casey said something about Boston and his work in the theater which was not widely discussed at the time, but which seems to me sound and reasonable: he said, in effect, that he had been merely the voice of the people, that the general Boston public did not want shows, or parts of shows, that offended against the moral convictions that they shared with him. In his defense, I believe he was right up to a certain point. Many, perhaps most Bostonians of his time shared his indignation at female nudity and at profanity on the stage. But not all of those who felt that way were theatergoers.

If this is correct, then Casey was acting for a majority who did *not* patronize the plays he deplored, and acting against that *minority* who were, and are, regular playgoers. Also, and this is not a mere matter of speculation, he was acting most of the time alone: offering his judgments and issuing his orders as a lone, fallible individual. He was behaving as a dictator, and that is gravely and grossly wrong. No one man, however knowledgeable or compassionate—and Casey, in my experience, was a kindly, sympathetic person—knows enough to set himself up as a judge without appeal in any sphere. Not even a drama critic.

Nobody knows, or is ever likely to know, the full extent of the cuts and alterations made by John Casey at previews provided for his inspection in New York, or after performances presented here. Most of his surgery was performed in private, and there is no written record; there never was. At the Old Howard in the burlesque days, managers complied only when Casey was watching. Theater people insist they have seen a signaling device that was used by the Howard box-office staff to warn the comics and the strippers that he was coming and to cut out the rough stuff; when the signal blinked a warning bulb in the footlight trough, the girls kept their clothes on and all the bananas in the bunch spoke politely. Otherwise, what Casey said was accepted as law, and the public got to hear about it only when producers who were genuinely concerned—or perhaps looking for publicity—protested.

*Mayor John F. Fitzgerald (center) 1906-07, 1910-13 (with arm raised) at a Red Sox baseball game.*

Plays were sometimes kept out of our theaters because the producers or the authors refused to accept the cuts our censor might make. "The Children's Hour," for example, by Lillian Hellman, wasn't booked for Boston. It is a beautiful play, and a discreet one, but our censor was indignant because in it an evil child whispers to a gullible guardian that her lady teachers are unholily in love. Nobody out front could hear the words, but little censors have big ears. Eugene O'Neill withheld "The Iceman Cometh" in 1947 because he refused to run the risk of having his text mutilated by a censor. Meanwhile, Casey and his followers had forced Louis Calhern, in "Life with Father," to substitute "Oh, Gad" for "Oh, God," Clarence Day's favorite expletive, and had required Will Geer to change Jeeter Lester's frequent "By God and by Jesus!" to something that sounded like "By Gad and by Cheese!"

Ironically, certain plays that exercised playgoers and even critics in other cities were allowed to play here without alteration or interference: "Ghosts," for instance. In Europe, Henrik Ibsen's drama created a scandal on its first production. In 1891, one London critic called it a "sewer," "an open drain." In Boston, it was performed without official protest at the Tremont Theater on April 18, 1894; for two matinees at the Hollis Street Theater thirteen years later; in a Russian production at the Park Theater in 1908 (with Nazimova as the maid Regina); at the Opera House at a matinee December 3, 1923, with Eleanora Duse starring (in Italian, of course); and at the Park Theater beginning March 21, 1927, with the great Mrs. Fiske as Mrs. Alving.

None of these performances seemed to cause any official action. It was not until 1935 that the play attracted municipal concern. When it opened at the Colonial Theater on November 25, Mayor Frederick W. Mansfield was in the audience, serving as his own censor. Afterward, he let it be known that he considered it "filthy" and "immoral." But he

*Mayor Malcolm E. Nichols 1926-29.*

allowed it to continue unaltered in a production that starred Nazimova, and which subsequently became a great New York success.

On January 15 of that same year Mansfield had banned Sean O'Casey's "Within the Gates," which had played in London and in New York with critical approval, because of the protests of two Jesuit fathers, the Reverends Terrence L. Connolly and Russell M. Sullivan, supported by the Methodist Bishop Charles Wesley Burns. They objected that it was "drenched with sex and written to point out the futility of religion." He agreed. In that play, which would seem to me highly religious in spirit, a bishop is represented as having become, in his seminary days, the father of an illegitimate child. He is at no point made to seem wicked, or less than repentant. He is a symbolic figure, not an individual. But he was a bishop, and that caused the trouble. "Within the Gates" did not play Boston.

The censorship action that caused the greatest uproar occurred in 1929 when the Theater Guild was refused permission to present Eugene O'Neill's "Strange Interlude" in Boston. In this case, another mayor was involved. It was Mayor Malcolm E. Nichols, not city censor John M. Casey, who decided the play was unacceptable and refused all appeals by the producers, the Theater Guild, to relent. Nichols saw the play in New York and indicated that certain language in it was offensive. Later, he refused to answer petitions by the directors of the Guild to specify what his objections were, and was silent in the face of their appeals and their offers to make any cuts he might require. He refused to answer their letters and telegrams. So, for fear of being closed down after a single performance, they took the play to Quincy, where it was presented in a movie theater on September 30, 1929; it was given a clean bill of health by the mayor of that city, who attended with his sister and with a number of clergymen.

Nine acts long, innovative in its use of "asides" to represent what the characters are thinking as opposed to what they are saying, "Strange Interlude" is about a woman's struggle for fulfillment. Nina Leeds, whose father limits her life, marries a good man but loves another. When she comes to believe that there is insanity in her husband's family, she has his baby aborted and later bears a son to her lover—and passes this boy off as her legitimate son. The play is not a light entertainment, and it may be that its nine long acts might have been cut to four or five, but it was in its day extraordinary in its psychological revelations. Nobody ever admitted it, least of all Mayor Nichols, but it was the abortion that really caused the ban. "Strange Interlude" is not likely to corrupt any morals. In Quincy, the notoriety brought a great many highschool students into the balconies, palpitant with excitement; after listening for two or

three hours, they were completely puzzled and bored, and left.

John Casey insisted afterward that "Strange Interlude" had not been banned; the Guild, he said, could have brought it to Boston. However, if the mayor, the police commissioner, and the chief justice of the municipal court decided that it was offensive, they could not only have closed it, but could have taken away the license of the Hollis Street Theater.

It is interesting to read the newspaper reports of religious and political attitudes toward "Strange Interlude," which were generally vehement, but varied. Bishop Samuel G. Babcock of the Protestant Episcopal Church headed a committee of Protestant clergymen who circularized their colleagues of many denominations, endorsing the mayor's stand and asking all ministers who agreed with him to speak from their pulpits. The *Pilot*, the official newspaper of the Catholic archdiocese, reported that "the Catholics of Boston are . . . plainly disgusted . . . and commend the fearless stand of the municipal authorities." On the other hand, the Reverend Raymond A. Chapman, vicar of St. Stephen's Episcopal Church, insisted that "neither the Mayor nor the Boston clergymen supporting him are in the least competent to censor plays." He insisted that "the play is a clean play."

Mayor McGrath of Quincy praised the play. John F. Fitzgerald, former mayor of Boston, admitting he had neither read nor seen it, said: "I think Boston is being made ridiculous. A play that has won the Pulitzer Prize, and that has been shown in the principal intelligent cities of the world, should be given a show here. The fuss over its showing in Boston is more like the action of a hick town than a metropolitan city." (Parenthetically, during the administration of Mayor Fitzgerald, in 1911, a play called "The Easiest Way" was forbidden entrance to Boston. For a further point of interest, Fitzgerald was a Democrat and Nichols a Republican. You know, and I know, that politics has no bearing in these cases, but I insert these facts for the record. . . . Also for the record, Malcolm E. Nichols was neither Irish nor Catholic, but a white Anglo-Saxon

*Eugene O'Neill.*

Protestant. So was one of his two closest associates, Charles H. Innes, who was unofficially considered the "afternoon mayor"; his other intimate, Ernest Goulston—the "night mayor"—was of the Jewish faith.)

Since the "Strange Interlude" interlude and the later cases of "Within the Gates" and "The Children's Hour," new regulations and court decisions and public actions have made censorship of the John Casey and Malcolm Nichols kind impossible. For breaking down the censorship, the Civil Liberties Union deserves most credit, though there have been other forces and factors at play, among them notable changes in public attitudes and what is tediously called "the new permissiveness."

With Reuben Goodman (now Judge Goodman) as counsel, the Civil Liberties Union took effective

*Judith Anderson as Nina Leeds in the Quincy, Mass. production of "Strange Interlude."*

steps against stage censorship when Edward Albee's play "Who's Afraid of Virginia Woolf?" came under the censor's displeasure. When Albee agreed to eliminate certain words, he was chided in print by Kevin Kelly, drama critic of the *Globe*. Defending his action, he revealed a secret clause in Boston theater contracts under which all such alterations had been mandatory.

Three years earlier, officials of the C.L.U. had acquired copies of a letter addressed to the manager of the Shubert Theater, Alice McCarthy, in which censor Richard J. Sinnott had ordered her to make eight changes in dialogue, lyrics, and actions in a comedy called "Lock Up Your Daughters." In act one, he ordered her to "please delete or revise line in which 'two gay blades' sing to 'wench' . . . 'lay her under the table or lay her under the sheets'"; in the same act, the words 'whore' and 'bastards' must be eliminated"—or else—and "in

same act please delete in its entirety bed scene involving Mrs. Squeezem and Ramble." These deletions were to be made at once, on the evening of the day, May 4, 1960, when the letter was hand-delivered to the manager, and it was stressed by the licensing chief that "these deletions are necessary if the play is to continue in the city of Boston."

Nobody in or out of the Civil Liberties Union considered "Lock Up Your Daughters" a master-work of the drama, or even a very good comedy of bawdry. But Mr. Sinnott's high-handed tone suggested that he was exercising arbitrarily power that under the law he did not have. C.L.U. objectors protested to Mayor John F. Collins that Massachusetts statutes of 1908, amended in 1915 and then in 1938, conferred theater "censorship" power on a board of three city officials: the mayor, the police commissioner, and, at this time, a member of the city art commission; also that precensorship of any productions by individual or board was no longer legally justifiable.

This carefully documented protest led to no positive action, but the revelation in 1963 of the previously secret rider to contracts signed by all producers and theater managers started a new battle that ended stage censorship in Boston. The rider had been introduced into the contract by Walter R. Milliken, then censor for James M. Curley, presumably with Curley's support. In listing the things that could not be said or done by actors and entertainers, it demonstrated in unforgettable language the kind of thinking behind Boston censorship. This is how it read:

Attention is called that the following has been adopted by the authorities of Boston in reference to theatrical performances and the party of the second part agrees to the following: 1) Dialogues, gestures and songs (especially parodies), language or conversation of any kind which are directly or by double meaning obscene or lascivious and intended to suggest sexual relations are to be eliminated. 2) The performers must be confined entirely to the stage. This especially prohibits female performers whether artists or chorus,

from using the aisles or passageways of the theater during their act. 3) Females prohibited from appearing upon the stage in [sic] legs bare, exception to this only permitted upon the authority of the Mayor or licensing committee. 4) Wearing of one piece union suits by females, where simply used to want to display the figure as in living pictures is prohibited. 5) The portrayal of a dope fiend by either sex, wherein the act of taking a hypodermic injection, the inhaling or eating of dope, or the use of dope in any manner intended to show the effects upon the human being is forbidden. 6) All forms of muscle dancing by either sex is prohibited. This includes every dance which contains suggestive or repulsive contortions of the human body. 7) The use of profanity will not be permitted. 8) The portrayal of a moral pervert or sex degenerate is not permitted.''

It was under section 7 that Richard J. Sinnott acted against "Who's Afraid of Virginia Woolf?" In a letter to Saul Kaplan, manager of the Colonial Theater, Mr. Sinnott wrote: "It is requested that all use of the Lord's name wherever it appears in the context of the play be deleted . . . this irreverent use of the Lord's name, in one form or another, appears at least nine additional times. In addition to deleting the word 'Jesus,' it is requested that the expression 'for Christ's sake' also be eliminated wherever it appears. It should be noted that the expressions 'Jesus,' 'Jesus Christ' and 'Christ' are used in reverence by millions of Christians and the abuse of these names are [sic] highly offensive."

Showing how things have changed in Boston, the same Richard Sinnott, discussing publicly the matter of censorship at the Boston Public Library on May 12, 1977, himself used the name of Jesus profanely to describe his indignation about the language of a movie called "Slapshot." He said, "Now 'Slapshot' is rated R—restricted; that means if you are under eighteen you must be accompanied by an adult. Have any of you seen 'Slapshot'? Jesus! there's a . . . there's a . . . I'm a father. I have kids who play hockey; I would be ashamed to

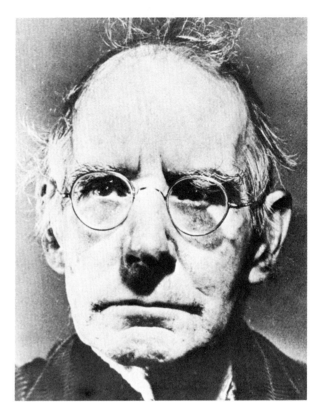

*Sean O'Casey.*

go see that movie with my kids. That's how bad it is. . . .''

In 1963, however, under section 7 of the rider, "Jesus" had to go, though it is interesting to note that in his letter to manager Kaplan, Mr. Sinnott "requested" the deletion, where in "Lock Up Your Daughters" he had been peremptory. (By way of another parenthesis, this matter of profanity was particularly sensitive in Boston because of Catholic sentiments, which the licensing chief was expressing in support of his order, or request. All Protestants revere or at least respect the name of Jesus. Male Catholic parishioners of Boston and other American cities were for many years organized in "Holy Name Societies" whose explicit purpose was to make sure that that particular name was used only with reverence, never profanely. This was never mentioned in print because it involved sensitive religious beliefs, but attempts to impose

*James Michael Curley.*

*Mayor Frederick W. Mansfield 1934-37.*

this Christian concept on audiences that consisted more and more of nonbelievers, among them an increasing number of Jewish playgoers, was a private but increasing source of friction.)

In any case, the Civil Liberties Union took up once again the fight against stage censorship and particularly against the rider, which constituted an agreed-upon precensorship, and on the long-since developed power of the licensing chief. The first letter of protest to Mayor Collins, signed by Albert R. Beisel, Jr., as chairman of the executive committee, and Reuben Goodman as chairman of the censorship committee, was written on April 3, 1963, five months before the "Virginia Woolf" incident. When the Libertarians received, on September 27, a copy of the rider, they began to exert further pressure on developing their contention that Mr. Sinnott was acting illegally.

John F. Collins was a good mayor, one of a

rather remarkable group of politicians who have done much to redeem Boston from the mal- and misfeasance of some of their predecessors while trying to cope with the apathy, the lassitude, and the incompetence of some of their fellow servants. As mayor, he had other things on his mind; as a politician, he was not eager to get into the area of censorship because of the undercurrents of racial and religious tension. He hesitated—no, let's put it this way: he stalled. Finally, however, he found a way to preserve his own image while acting for freedom: he disowned, and thereby in effect cancelled the rider by blaming it on Jim Curley.

His letter to Howard S. Whiteside, then chairman of the Civil Liberties Union of Massachusetts, dated April 8, 1965, began as follows: "Your letter was received in this office while I was in Washington on official business. The rider which you refer to between Boston theater owners and New York producers did not originate with this administration and no such restrictions are imposed by this administration." He went on to suggest that the citizens of Boston "are entitled to be protected from prurient and pornographic material and we enlist your cooperation in this endeavor and the protec-

*John M. Casey, Boston's "city censor" for 28 years, until 1932.*

Virginia Woolf?" played Boston at the Shubert, in a second production, uncensored. This time the actors were not forced to substitute Mary Magdalen's name for that of Jesus, as the original players had elected to do in a spirit of playful, but entirely legal, protest. Since then, there have been two cases when stage productions have attracted attention from the now-caponed censor; he found certain ways to cope with both while adhering to the new rules.

On May 3, 1966, he attended a performance in the Hotel Touraine Theater of a play called "The Investigation," written by Rosalyn Drexler and produced by the Theater Company of Boston. He found some of the language offensive, which indeed it was, and decided it was obscene, which is a matter of opinion. This time, instead of writing a stern letter to the producers as he had done so

tion of the civil liberties of all parties concerned."

That official statement meant the end of the stage censorship that had plagued Boston since 1904, when John M. Casey began to exceed his legal authority and became, instead of a mere messenger of the mayor, a dictator of taste for an art he didn't even enjoy

When word of Mayor Collins's action got around the loudest voice of protest came from a pulpit: not Catholic, but Congregational. At "Brimstone Corner," in the grand old Park Street Congregational Church at the foot of Beacon Hill, the Reverend Harold J. Ockenga declared: "It is disgraceful that we are degenerating so fast in the name of civil liberties. . . . I am in favor of censorship and will do anything I can to have it retained."

Even before the mayor's official action, the air had been cleared so that "Who's Afraid of

*Lillian Hellman.*

*Richard J. Sinnott, the last of the Boston "city censors."*

often in the past, he notified the Boston police, who sent Officer Willis D. Saunders, Jr. to the next performance. In municipal court on May 20, Saunders listed words he found obscene and described a love scene he found to be offensive under the law. Elijah M. Adlow, chief justice of the Boston Municipal Court, listened to the patrolman and to representatives of the Theater Company of Boston for just ten minutes, then decided that there was no "obscenity" of any consequence and no "lewdness"; in dismissing the case he suggested, "Let's not make a mountain out of a molehill." Mr. Sinnott's procedure in this instance was even more significant than the judge's finding. Instead of acting arbitrarily, ordering out of the play what he as an individual, found offensive, he

had given the producers their day in court, had allowed them due process of law.

When "Hair" opened here at the Wilbur Theater on March 6, 1970, it was widely predicted that Mr. Sinnott would take some kind of action because of the nude scene. He did act, and succeeded in stopping the production for four weeks, but not for nudity or obscenity or lewdness. He objected to what he called "the desecration of the American flag," and in so doing brought in the district attorney's office.

"What I did object to," said Mr. Sinnott afterward "was not the nude scene . . . the nude scene was pathetic; there wasn't a beautiful body in the whole bunch . . . what I did take action against was the almost continuous desecration of the flag of the

United States, and I almost died fighting for that flag and I think I have the right to speak up to protect the flag of the country I love. And I did this through the office of the district attorney, and the practice was ended immediately.''

Despite this new attitude on the part of the licensing chief, last in the long line that began with czar John M. Casey and protected from harm by a civil service appointment, the reputation of Boston censorship was still so formidable in 1974 that producer Kermit Bloomgarden decided against opening Peter Shaffer's ''Equus'' here. His fear of official action was shared by the Jujamcyn Corporation, owners of the Colonial Theater; they refused to guarantee him against legal actions, so he abandoned the idea of a tryout here and opened in New York after previews. When he did send a company to Boston, however, to open at the Wilbur Theater November 18, 1975, there was no censor action, no police action, and no letters to the manager.

Here was a strong drama that violated just about every one of the old taboos, and went so far in one scene as to strip a young man and woman naked, attempting to have sexual intercourse. This with part of the audience seated on the stage in bleachers, only a few feet away from the actors. Casey would have raged. Censor Walter R. Milliken would have brandished the secret rider and demanded action; the young Richard Sinnott would have dispatched by hand a stern letter of orders to the manager. But the Sinnott of 1976, tamed by new rules and by what he considers ''the new mores, the new permissiveness,'' enjoyed the play, made no comments, no ''suggestions,'' and in effect indicated that the old order has changed. All official censorship in Boston died that night, seventy-one years after John M. Casey started it and two centuries after the Declaration of Independence.

*The second Toy Theater, opened in 1914 on Dartmouth Street opposite the side door of the Copley Plaza Hotel, became the Copley. In 1922, it was turned around to face the Stuart Street extension and was expanded.*

# CHAPTER VIII

## THE TRAGEDIANS OF THE CITY – AND COMICS, TOO

In Boston, we have had our own acting companies from the beginning, recruited to provide our play-goers, not those of New York or any other city, with the best in dramatic entertainment.

We had one when the first "moral entertainments" were presented at the New Exhibition Room; we had them all through the nineteenth century and into the twentieth. We still have a few. But the nature and composition of these troupes has changed drastically, as the theater of the United States has changed.

The records are not clear about the company at the New Exhibition Room, but it seems certain they were recruited from the pool of English actors who had been playing up and down the East Coast since 1751: some seem to have been former members of the "American Company," whose founders were Lewis and William Hallam. In any case, they were repertory players, capable of presenting such classics as "Romeo and Juliet" and "Othello," or of putting on variety shows, all under the guise of moral entertainments.

At the Federal Street Theater, the players were also capable of presenting the classics, including Shakespeare, and whatever English plays were available, and when stars like George Frederick Cooke began to arrive from England, followed by the first Americans of star rank, they were willing, able, and ready to act in their support. For more than a hundred years, this was the way the resident theaters of Boston and other American cities operated. By themselves, the actors put on whatever plays were current or popular, or seemed likely to please. When the stars came to visit, they took over all the supporting roles.

When Forrest arrived in "Metamora," they knew that by heart; also "Hamlet," and "Othello"; if he brought in a new one, they had to learn new parts and learn them fast, under special handicaps. In those years, before the copyright laws had been developed, the visiting stars might be unwilling to send a complete script ahead. Instead, they would dispatch a stage manager with "sides" that included the actors' own roles, but only cue lines to indicate what Edwin Forrest would say. In this way, the Boston actors would be unable to transcribe the material and use it, perhaps under a new title, in another theater.

Such theaters as the first and second Boston, the Tremont, the Haymarket, and the Howard Athenaeum engaged their acting companies in the spring or summer for the season that began in September, and although they retained some from one year to the next, usually made many cast changes. The Boston Museum, while following the same production policies, began soon after its new building was opened in 1846 to retain many of its principal players year after year and some of these actors and actresses developed their own loyal and admiring public.

William Warren was one. Warren was recognized as a leading American actor, admired and respected in the professional world by such stars as Edwin Booth. He joined the company on August 27, 1847, and remained for thirty-six years with only one season away with a troupe of his own. When he retired, some of the great men of Boston gathered to honor him at a dinner.

Another regular, dear to Bostonians, born Mary Ann Farley in England, and known here as Mrs. J. R. Vincent, acted at the Museum from 1852 until her death in 1887, skipping just one season to

*Mrs. J. R. Vincent, great and beloved star of the Boston Museum. The Vincent Memorial Hospital and the Vincent Club were founded in memory of her private charities.*

appear with Edwin Forrest in Baltimore. Mrs. Vincent was not only a fine actress, she was a kindly woman whose private charities led after her death to the founding of a hospital. The Vincent Memorial Hospital and the Vincent Club, whose members put on a show annually for the benefit of that hospital, are living memorials to the esteem in which she was held.

The stock company at the Museum closed in 1893. That at the Boston Theater had ended eight years earlier, giving way, as all these resident companies did throughout the country, to touring shows: plays or musicals traveling intact with their own players, their own scenery and costumes. The stars were still on the road, playing Boston as they

played every city, big or small, for a week or two or a one-night stand—for the American theater was national then—but they no longer needed the resident players.

In 1915, "The Birth of a Nation," the significant American feature film, was presented here at the Tremont Theater and at the same time in similar playhouses across the country, and the silent film industry of Hollywood began to grow into a great and pervasive institution, spreading its pictures through the world. Twelve years later, Al Jolson's "The Jazz Singer" was shown here at the new Beacon Theater, on Tremont Street opposite the site of the Boston Museum, which had long since been razed. Within five years, the last of Boston's stock companies closed down.

In the meantime, new local companies had begun to appear, influenced by the little theater movement of Europe, which had first attracted attention when Andre Antoine opened his Théâtre Libre in Paris in 1887, presenting the new and radical dramas of Ibsen and Strindberg. The movement spread to Berlin and London, and led to the founding in 1896 of the Moscow Art Theater, and, in Dublin in 1899, of the Irish Literary Theater, which five years later became the Abbey Theater.

In 1891, as I have already mentioned, a group of Bostonians produced a radically realistic drama by James A. Herne called "Margaret Fleming," and announced publicly they hoped to create "an American Théâtre Libre." They didn't make it; but when the Abbey Theater played here at the Plymouth Theater in 1911, and William Butler Yeats, its great founding father, lectured at Harvard on the new movements, a group of Bostonians led by Mrs. Lyman Gale and including the poet Amy Lowell organized the first little theater in America. They called it the Toy Theater, because it was tiny, and they created a playhouse by making over a stable at 16 Lime Street. There, opening January 1, 1912, they put on the first of several of the new dramas of Europe.

In the meantime, Professor George Pierce Baker of Harvard had been agitating for a new theater. Baker had been to Europe, had seen most of the experimenters at work, knew their playwriting

techniques and their innovations in lighting and scenic design and was fascinated. He got together with Henry Lee Higginson, who was willing in 1905 to help finance in Boston a theater that would operate on the same level of excellence as the Boston Symphony Orchestra and the Museum of Fine Arts. Higginson would stay in the background, and did.

A young enthusiast named Winthrop Ames joined in this project, took over the Castle Square Theater in 1904, and began to put on plays that were not necessarily ground-breakers but that were handsomely produced, and in his second year offered a Shakespeare festival that created a stir of admiration. Two years later, Ames went to Europe to study the new playhouses, and came back here ready to build in Boston. He had acquired the site for a perfect little theater. Then he changed his mind, and accepted instead a call to New York to start a company there in a big playhouse called the New Theater. He later opened in 45th Street the Little Theater, which still stands though its earliest mission was unfulfilled.

An actor named John Craig took over the management of the Castle Square Theater in 1911, and established a connection with Harvard and with Baker's ideas of a new American drama by annually offering a prize of $500 and a production to students of Baker's playwriting course—English 47. He produced these "Harvard Prize Plays" in 1911, 1912, 1913, 1915-1916, and 1917, some of them for substantial runs, and although none proved to be the great American drama everyone was looking for, two were subsequently taken to Broadway, and one, "Believe Me, Xanthippe," by Baker's student Frederick W. Ballard, got to be a long-run New York success with John Barrymore starred.

While Baker's students were thus creating a reputation for their professor and themselves, and beginning, at any rate, to reflect something of the American scene in their dramas, the Toy Theater was in business at a new address on Dartmouth Street. Later it was enlarged, moved backward, and prepared as the home of two successive professional companies, whose directors aimed to provide Boston with plays of some substance, both

*William Warren, who spent most of his long professional career in the stock company at the Boston Museum.*

European and American, with professional actors. In the stable, the actors had been amateurs. At the new playhouse the first players were from the same group, with a few professionals added. Now, in 1914, with seven hundred seats to fill, they needed professional assistance. A year later, an Australian actor named Henry Jewett, who had been trying to create a resident company here, took over the Toy Theater and began to make Boston theatrical history.

Henry Jewett wanted what Hamlin Garland had wanted when he put on "Margaret Fleming" in Chickering Hall back in 1891; what George Pierce Baker and Henry Lee Higginson and Winthrop Ames had hoped to create here; what the original amateurs of the Toy Theater had hoped to achieve;

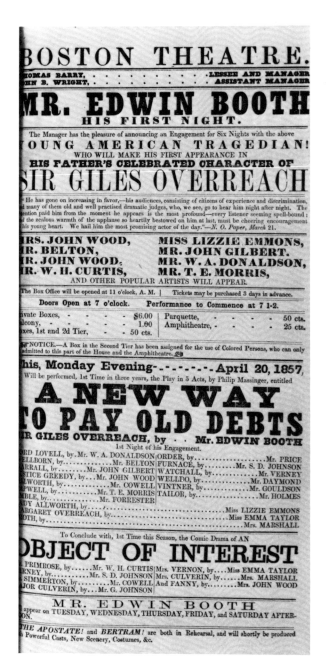

*above: Edwin Booth began his rise to stardom in Boston, at the second Boston Theater, in a repertory of new and old plays. Note that the program advertises him as appearing as "his father's celebrated character," Sir Giles Overreach. At that time, in 1857, Junius Brutus Booth's fame overreached that of Edwin.*

and what the Castle Square Theater, by this time, was beginning to neglect in favor of conventional comedies and melodramas. His ambition was to establish a first-rate resident company of actors, presenting plays better than those of the commercial theater for Bostonians. He very nearly made it on a large scale. But he, too, was eventually done in by the motion pictures.

At the Copley, working now with professionals, he was so successful that in 1922 he had the playhouse pulled apart—literally—and relocated on Stuart Street. Drays drawn by many horses drew the building back from Dartmouth Street into the lot behind, then split it in two, moving the front half out to face Stuart Street and linking the back half up behind it; then building and inserting a middle section that increased the capacity of the theater to nearly two thousand. Here he put on dramas of some merit until some of his actors revolted to form a separate company. Then backed by some of Boston's most eminent citizens, he drew up the plans for a new playhouse.

On November 10, 1925, he opened the Repertory Theater of Boston in a magnificent new building on Huntington Avenue opposite Symphony Hall, with a production of Sheridan's "The Rivals," and with every expectation that "America's first civic playhouse," as it was called, would become a great and permanent Boston institution. Two years later, at a hundred-dollar-a-plate dinner in the Copley Plaza Hotel, with national publicity and enthusiasm, Jewett and his friends launched a campaign to raise additional funds for the new theater, which had cost more to build than he had been able to find.

Bostonians were pleased with the theater, but the new movies—the "talkies"— were taking away the audiences by the hundreds and the thousands, and when Jewett died in 1928, the Repertory Theater of Boston was in bad trouble. Two years later, having been unable to reverse the downward spiral and to find funds to pay off the indebtedness, his widow closed it. "You can't run a repertory company without a subsidy," said Mrs. Frances Jewett, speaking for so many who followed her husband's lead and are still following it today.

E. E. Clive, who had taken over most of Jewett's company in 1924, kept them going at the Copley until 1932, when he, too, was obliged to close in the face of the talkies.

The Castle Square stock company had gone under early in the twenties, suffering from the same dire competition; in 1932, the year John Craig died, the old building (which had since been rechristened the Arlington) was razed, and the furnishings had been sold at auction.

There had been a number of other stock companies in Boston, and several, all professional, in such suburban cities as Somerville, Malden, and Quincy. Downtown, on Bowdoin Street, the Bowdoin Square Theater had a resident troupe in the early years of the twentieth century, playing not the advanced dramas of Europe but the conventional melodramas and slight comedies of earlier Broadway seasons. Uptown, beginning in 1912, Chickering Hall was converted into the St. James Theater, which followed the same pattern and, like the old Castle Square and the Boston Museum before it, and the Copley under Jewett and Clive, attracted faithful audiences who got to know and admire actors and actresses who appeared in many plays during several successive seasons.

From 1912-1914, Alfred Lunt was a beginning member of the Castle Square stock company; he had been sent here by his parents in Wisconsin to go to school at what was then called the Emerson College of Oratory. He visited the school, took a look around, walked over to Castle Square, asked for a job, and was put to work. John Craig, who operated the Castle Square during its most productive years, was its male star. His co-star was his wife, Mary Young. Both were beloved and faithfully supported by playgoers of their era, until the movies became too attractive. At the Copley, Jewett was an attraction. Later, E. E. Clive and such actors and actresses as Rosalind Russell, Walter Pidgeon, and for a while Morris Carnovsky, had their partisans. At the St. James, Viola Roach, an admirable actress, had a personal following, admiring and devoted. But the stock companies were doomed, and it would take a little while before new groups of amateurs and professionals

would begin again the perennial drive to provide Boston with an acting company of its own.

Four years after the closing of Jewett's Repertory Theater, the Federal Theater of the Works Progress Administration moved into that admirable playhouse with a company of actors who were, in some cases at least, out-of-work professionals, and began to put on plays for Bostonians as other, similar companies were doing in other parts of the country. They weren't very good in Boston. By this time in the American theater, most of the good performers who hadn't gone to Hollywood were living, or barely living, in New York, where the American legitimate theater had long since been concentrated; they would literally rather starve there than flourish here. So, with a few exceptions, those who acted here were second- or third-raters. However, they were the Boston representatives of a project that was heroic in concept, and that, if the wrong politicians had not got hold of it, might well have developed into a national theater.

The idea behind it was humane and decent: to furnish work in their own field for people of the theater; to pay them not for loafing but for performing; to make it possible for them to continue in action and to be paid for it. The salaries were tiny, even by standards of the day—$26 a week for actors—but the benefit to the theater was great and the possibilities unlimited. In New York, unfortunately, some of the most gifted theater people of America dared to put on productions that attracted the ire of some of the most obtuse members of Congress, and the entire project, including of course the Boston company, was liquidated.

One spinoff from this Federal Theater was a semiprofessional company called the Tributary Theater of Boston, directed by a talented and ambitious Bostonian named Eliot Duvey. Duvey's aims were high: he wanted, as many before and since wanted, to create a resident theater that would produce the best plays of the world repertory on a small budget. He was handicapped—here again, like so many similar dreamers—by an inability to raise any substantial sums of money, and by a failure to find actors and actresses who were good enough to play effectively, in competition with the

players of the commercial theaters. His achievement, and that of those who worked with him, was keeping alive the concept of a Boston resident theater for the kinds of plays that the commercial theater, by this time, had all but abandoned. (His Tributary Theater troupers operated most of the time in what was then called New England Mutual Hall, now New England Life Hall, on Clarendon Street.)

In the same period, Edwin Burr Pettet, who later became chairman of the theater arts department at Brandeis, created the New England Repertory Theater. His ideas and ideals were similar to Duvey's, his resources even smaller. He kept his company going in tiny theaters on Beacon Hill from 1938 till 1945, before finally giving up. The war had taken away his best actors.

After the war, for four years we got a bright and lively company, not in Boston but in Cambridge, handy to the Harvard Square subway, located in old Brattle Hall where Professor Baker had once thought of starting a theater. The Brattle Theater Company began at Harvard in 1947, when an undergraduate named Jerome Kilty—who would write, some years later, the play "Dear Liar," in which Katharine Cornell ended her career—decided that the Harvard Dramatic Club was not sufficiently adventurous for him, and wondered how many other Harvard men back from the war, older than some of their classmates, might be interested in getting together to act. During the war, stationed in England, he had seen the repertory companies of London, and had been fired with the idea that they might be matched over here.

Jerry Kilty put an ad in the *Harvard Crimson* one day in 1947 requesting all veterans of the war who might have ideas similar to his to get together for conversation. So many responded that he would have been overwhelmed, except that he was young, talented, and ambitious. Then and there, he and his respondents organized what they called the

*Bill for the first American performance of Gilbert and Sullivan's "H.M.S. Pinafore," at the Boston Museum, November 25, 1878.*

Veterans' Theater Workshop, and a few months later in Sanders Theater put on a production of Shakespeare's "King Richard II," with Kilty as the king, and with all kinds of skills and talents apparent. A year later, since some of their daddies had a few dollars, they bought old Brattle Hall and became a professional resident acting company.

Their Brattle Theater Company produced in the period between 1948 and 1952 many of the classics of the world repertory, English, American, and continental. They offered Shaw, Congreve. Shakespeare, and Molière, among others, and they did almost everything by themselves, from acting to directing to designing, painting, and building scenery; and sewing costumes. For some of the major roles in their principal plays they brought in outsiders: Cyril Ritchard for Restoration comedy; Zero Mostel, whom hardly anyone knew in those days, for Molière; and, from England, Hermione Gingold.

In the beginning, so much of what they did was bright and promising and so many Greater Bostonians were so delighted to have a repertory company that they were not only praised but, I am afraid, seriously overpraised. Then, as they proceeded they were handicapped by the kind of

*Castle Square Theater (1894-1933) on Tremont Street at Chandler—home of stock companies, opera, touring plays.*

problems that plague all such companies. For one, they had to keep going week after week once they opened their seasons. And they found it difficult with a limited pool of actors and designers to get all their productions in good shape in time.

Also, without subsidies they had to rely on the box office and that was a particularly tricky business, because their playhouse seated fewer than four hundred people. They found that most of their audience stayed away early in the week, then came on strong on the weekends. Sometimes they were almost empty on Mondays and Tuesdays and then turning people away on Fridays and Saturdays. At that time, the "blue laws" made it impossible to give performances on Sunday, which is now one of the most popular evenings for little theater companies like theirs. Again, because they had no financial cushion on which they could rest when times were hard, they were forced to close down failed productions overnight, and to substitute others with only four or five rehearsals. They were talented and ambitious, but after four years they were unable to continue; it became financially impossible.

At about this time, there was a new stirring in America, a new national movement at the grass roots for theaters that, like the old acting companies of the nineteenth century, would serve their own cities or their own areas. Their founders had ideas very like those of Jerry Kilty, but some of them had greater resources, and a few were more carefully organized. Some just had better luck. They began what came to be known as the "regional theater movement," which is now flourishing in at least thirty cities and which constitutes, at its best, a rich alternative to the commercial theater of Broadway.

Women were among the first movers and shakers in this national action. Nina Vance in Houston, Margo Jones in Dallas, and Zelda Fichandler in Washington, D. C., all created theaters that their communities could support. Later, under male leadership, others followed in Los Angeles, in San Francisco, St. Louis, Minneapolis (where Tyrone Guthrie organized and built the theater that bears his name), in New Haven, Hartford,

*John Craig, a Boston favorite in the early years of the twentieth century at the Castle Square Theater, where he frequently co-starred with Mary Young, his wife.*

Springfield, Providence, and Boston.

In November, 1957, a company of Boston University students who had been performing on Cape Cod found a long, bare room on the second floor of a building at 54 Charles Street, directly above a fish market. And there they opened Jean-Paul Sartre's play "No Exit," in an interesting performance. They called their theater the Charles Playhouse.

The next season, with Michael Murray now enlisted as artistic director, they turned professional and moved from Charles Street to take over and remodel a former nightclub which had been built as a church on Warrenton Street. In memory

of their beginnings they named it the Charles Playhouse, and in it, despite all sorts of hazards, they gave Boston its longest-lived regional theater, continuing until 1970.

Boston has had a number of other ventures of this kind, some lasting briefly, some running into the present. The Theater Company of Boston existed for years side by side with the Charles Playhouse Company and has sometimes used the Charles Playhouse building; it was, and still is, the brainchild of a man named David Wheeler. Mr. Wheeler began producing in 1963 in the old Hotel Bostonian on Boylston Street, in a makeshift theater that seated ninety-five people, with a company that included in its first plays Dustin Hoffman, who was so ambitious he insisted on playing two roles in one production.

In the period between 1963 and 1970, the Theater Company of Boston and the Charles Playhouse were able to co-exist; although their general aims were similar, their particular ambitions

*Mary Young.*

were somewhat different. The Charles was oriented toward a broad repertory of fine plays; the T.C.B. was concerned with the newer and more highly experimental dramas, such as those of Harold Pinter. The Charles audiences got to see not only the best of O'Neill, but some of the more adventurous plays of Brecht, among them, in 1966, "Galileo." The T.C.B. introduced Harold Pinter's "The Dwarfs" to America, sending part of its audience reeling.

The Charles Company was able, down through the years of its existence, to stay in one playhouse, which was and still is uncomfortable, but which has a good thrust stage and an atmosphere of intimacy. The Theater Company never got a permanent address; it has been moved from one tem-

*Henry Jewett, an Australian actor who in the period from 1915 till his death in 1928 operated a number of repertory companies in Boston.*

*The Repertory Theater of Boston, 264 Huntington Avenue, was opened in 1925 by Henry Jewett's repertory company. Closed five years later, it became a moviehouse, and in 1958 was taken over by Boston University.*

porary address to another, and Mr. Wheeler has found in the last few years that he needs big-name stars to get an audience in the halls and hallways where he is forced to play. For two successive years, Al Pacino came to Boston to star with the T.C.B. and he brought in the playgoers. In 1976, he agreed to play "Hamlet" then canceled, leaving them with a disrupted and broken season. In 1977, he said he would revive with them David Rabe's Vietnam war drama, "The Basic Training of Pavlo Hummel," but they must come to New York. That's what they did, with considerable success, but ironically this company still has no Boston playhouse. One of the newest of the resident theater companies is the Boston Repertory Theater, which is professional. They have a tiny playhouse of their own which they made over from an old recording studio on Boylston Place, in the downtown theater area, and they have managed to give more than forty productions since 1971, some of them effective, some amateurish.

*Charles Playhouse on Warrenton Street, built in 1843 as a church, designed by Asher Benjamin. Later it became a restaurant, and in 1947, the Charles Playhouse housing a resident company for fourteen years.*

# CHAPTER IX

## TRYOUTS AND TRIUMPHS: BROADWAY DOWNEAST

When Winthrop Ames, after two years of preparation here, decided to set up an ideal little theater in New York instead of Boston, he was pointing to the future; he understood that the trend of the theater, even then, was in the direction of New York as the central city, the hub of the theater wheel. When Harvard coolly rejected George Pierce Baker's request for a theater to house the original plays of his gifted dramatists and forced him in 1925 to establish one at Yale that drained away more talent, more of the men and women who were by that time beginning to renew the American theater, that was another sign: Boston was relinquishing its potential leadership in twentieth-century drama.

Although they came here to present all their plays, some of the stars of the nineteenth century had begun to think of success in the Park Theater of New York as most prestigious. At the beginning of the twentieth, a few were testing their new productions in other cities before exposing them to New York audiences. Ethel Barrymore opened "Captain Jinks of the Horse Marines" in Philadelphia, then took it to Broadway in 1901; she made sure it was ready before bringing it in. Earlier, a Bostonian named Charles H. Hoyt had discovered it could be advantageous to try out the new comedies he was beginning to write in small cities of New England and later in Boston before offering them to New Yorkers.

Hoyt was a columnist and critic for the old Boston *Post,* who had learned by firsthand observation that some dramatists were not great craftsmen and that there were those among them who welcomed a little assistance in revising weak scenes. So he assisted. He became an unofficial "play doctor" of shows at the Howard Athenaeum, then turned to creating his own comedies, found he had a flair for writing, and, what is just as important in popular comedy, for rewriting. He developed a regular pattern of producing his new plays in the spring in small cities; then closing down for the summer to rewrite scenes that hadn't worked; then a new tryout engagement in Jersey City in the fall; then, perhaps, Boston, and only after all this, New York.

Before Hoyt, other playwrights and play doctors had worked on revising and altering plays in production, but he was the father of the tryout system, which would become a vital part of the American commercial theater. Other authors of his time in the eighties and nineties, among them playwrights as talented as James A. Herne, worked to improve imperfect shows from one city to the next, hoping that they would have a hit eventually, Hoyt had the twentieth-century notion of preparing in Boston, or Jersey City, or Concord, N.H., specifically for New York, where, as he had discovered, the largest audiences were. On February 9, 1891, his comedy "A Trip to Chinatown" opened at the Boston Theater for two weeks of testing. Nine months later, having in the meantime improved it in other cities, he finally took it into the Madison Square Theater in New York where it ran for 657 performances, establishing a long-run record and proving to at least a few observers that "plays are not written, they are rewritten," and they had better be rewritten before they were exposed in New York.

*opposite: Tallulah Bankhead pours tea as Regina Giddens in "The Little Foxes," her greatest role.*

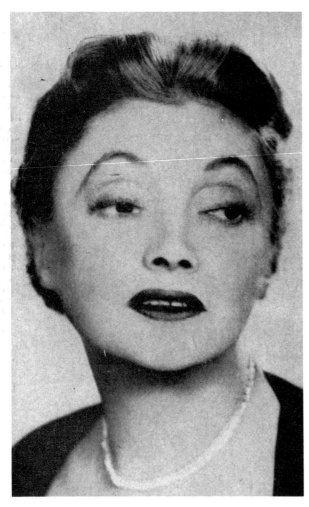

*Katharine Cornell in her final role, as Mrs. Patrick Campbell in "Dear Liar," with Brian Aherne, at the Wilbur Theater, Boston, where she gave the last performances of her career.*

WILBUR THEATRE — MAX MICHAELS, Manager

PROGRAM WEEK OF MAY 2, 1960

GUTHRIE McCLINTIC
in association with
S. HUROK
presents

Katharine                    Brian
CORNELL                    AHERNE

in

Jerome Kilty's

DEAR LIAR

A Comedy of Letters adapted for the stage from the correspondence of Mrs. Patrick Campbell and Bernard Shaw

Directed by
MR. KILTY

Decor by                          Lighting by
DONALD OENSLAGER          JEAN ROSENTHAL

Costumes by                    Incidental Music by
CECIL BEATON                  SOL KAPLAN

The message didn't get through to everyone, however, until after 1919, when a group of actors and actresses who were tired of being victimized by greedy producers and managers formed a union, the Actors' Equity Association, walked out on strike, and finally won certain concessions which made their profession a little less precarious while at the same time increasing greatly the cost of production.

Until the managers yielded, most of them with bad grace, actors had been required to rehearse as long as a director required, without pay; if he so desired, they might spend seven or eight weeks learning lines, old and new, while slowly starving to death. There were other abuses, some of them degrading and intolerable, for many of the men who ran the theaters of America at that time had the minds of Mafia dons. But the rehearsal pay became one important factor in the development during the twenties and thirties of the tryout pattern that Charles Hoyt had pioneered. Under the new agreement, actors were paid a token amount—as little as twenty dollars a week—for each of the first four weeks of rehearsal; after that, they went on full salaries. Rehearsal costs were not great in the

beginning, but the sums required increased after 1919, as the Actors' Equity Association gained in power. In any case, it was the requirement that all performers be paid full wages starting with the fifth week, whether the play was ready or not, that led to a new dependence on tryouts.

Established dramas, as for example those of playwrights like Shaw or Barrie or even Chekhov, and now perhaps Tennessee Williams, can sometimes be prepared in a month of rehearsals, for the text has long since been finalized and it only remains for the director to find a pattern of performance and coach good actors in it. But American plays of the twenties, thirties, and forties were mostly new, untested, and in many cases unperfected. Four weeks of rehearsal were not enough to find and perhaps eliminate errors in the text, the performances, the direction, and in such other vital arts as scenic, costume, and lighting design. So the

producers, being now afraid to present their productions in unfinished form in New York, took to the cities of the road—among them New Haven, Boston, and Philadelphia—and began there to revise and rewrite, to change actors who didn't measure up, to change scenery when it did not suit the play, to bring in play doctors, and, in hotel suites here and in other cities, to rewrite songs, scenes, and often entire acts, remaking plays and musicals too to insure eventual success on Broadway. That became the objective, and it still is: to revise, polish, repair, and perfect new plays, or new productions, using the audiences of Boston and other cities as more or less willing guinea pigs.

I have suggested that New York had long since become the major city among many where plays were produced, partly because of its growing prestige, and partly because it had the largest number of potential playgoers and therefore the

*Katharine Cornell as Elizabeth Barrett (Browning), her most successful role, in "The Barretts of Wimpole Street."*

# KATHARINE CORNELL
# GODFREY TEARLE
# Antony and Cleopatra

By WILLIAM SHAKESPEARE

*with*

### KENT SMITH      LENORE ULRIC

RALPH CLANTON      IVAN SIMPSON

Staged by GUTHRIE McCLINTIC

Settings by LEO KERZ        Music by PAUL NORDOFF
Women's Costumes by VALENTINA     Men's Costumes by JOHN BOYT

greatest financial rewards; longer runs were possible there, and that meant more money for everyone. Between 1915 and 1930 the importance of New York and the need to prepare productions carefully for Broadway success increased enormously, because of the sudden development of the silent movies and the talkies, and in the meantime, the increase in the power of the New York drama critics.

We had had movies since before the turn of the century. But until the presentation in 1915 at the Tremont Theater of "The Birth of a Nation," they had been a minor entertainment medium. "The Birth of a Nation" ran for a full evening, as long as a play; it was a successful new form of dramatic entertainment to match and compete with what now came to be known as "the legitimate theater," which is to say the theater of live plays and actors. In Boston, it shook up the people, stirred public indignation, led to a change of the Massachusetts statute on censorship, and, as it would do elsewhere, began to turn thousands and thousands of people to the new movies. Eight years later, the first talkie, "The Lights of New York," was accepted as a curiosity, but in 1927 Al Jolson's "The Jazz Singer," which was part silent and part sound, blew the silent-film industry apart. Within five years, all theaters had been converted to sound, all our stock companies and most of those in other parts of the country had been closed, and the American theater had been transformed in a great revolution of public taste.

Legitimate theaters were bought up and used for moviehouses, or in some cases, closed down as opposition to Hollywood. At the same time, new motion-picture "palaces" like the Metropolitan on Tremont Street were being erected: "deluxe houses," handsome in marble and gilt, with comfortable seats in contrast to those of the old playhouses; with polite ushers and treasurers, and in addition to feature films, their own symphony orchestras, providing entertainment for far less money than

opposite: *Katharine Cornell at the Wilbur Theater in Boston in "Antony and Cleopatra."*

the opposition. In 1925, a Boston playgoer could put down $3.30 for a ticket to the Shubert or Colonial, with a reserved seat which, if he was lucky or had influence, might be comfortable; or he could go to the Metropolitan to any one of four shows for seventy cents. And if he were greedy for entertainment, or too lazy to leave its opulent comfort, he could stay all day. Some enthusiasts, young and old, saw three or four successive shows.

This, of course, was happening all across the country. More and more playhouses were closing, and the legitimate theater was shrinking back to New York City as its only major producing and exhibiting center. It is estimated that there were more than four thousand theaters in the United States in 1900, some of them handsome and elaborate like our Colonial, some mere halls that could be adapted to any kind of entertainment, many of them called opera houses because down through the nineteenth century opera companies had played there, alternating with medicine shows, minstrels, "Tom" shows, and whatever. Now they were closing, one after another. In 1932, for a fair estimate, there were only about four hundred left in the entire country.

Seventy-five of those that remained were in New York; there were seven in Boston. That meant we could have some live drama, but all plays and musicals were written explicitly for New York and New York alone; the theater had ceased to exist as a great national enterprise and had become insular.

During this upheaval, the drama critics of New York had begun to gain a new and unique power, and this would become a factor in the making, exhibiting, and booking of plays and in the further development of the tryout system. Until 1915, because of the power of the syndicates that owned the theaters and spent large amounts of money advertising in the newspapers, drama critics of New York were under pressure to evaluate what they saw in friendly, or noncommittal, terms; others, who were honest enough but too erudite, or too "literary," were unread by the general public. In 1914, the New York *Times* appointed a young crime reporter, Alexander Woollcott, as its play

critic. A year later the Shubert brothers who owned most of the theaters in New York, protested one of his unfavorable reviews and banned him. The publisher backed him up; he refused to cover their shows and his paper denied the Shuberts advertising space.

The battle over this banning lasted a year, and when it was over the Shuberts had won technically, but the situation had changed drastically. Critics of the Manhattan dailies, except for the *Times*, could still expect to be banned if they offended Lee or J. J. Shubert, and many of them were until 1942 when the U.S. Supreme Court upheld a state law that made it illegal to keep out of a theater anyone who had a ticket and who behaved reasonably well. But men who now began to write criticism along with Woollcott on the New York dailies were no longer afraid, and what is more, were now being recruited by their publishers as he had been: not for erudition, but for the ability to write freely and interestingly for anyone who might want to buy a ticket to a show.

Some, like Brooks Atkinson of the *Times,* and John Mason Brown, knew a great deal about the theater. Others, like Heywood Broun, were drawn from such other departments as sports because they could write well. Most were bold and courageous. And as the theater of New York became in effect the theater of America, they became a set of stern and incorruptible judges to whom the public turned as to oracles for final judgments. By 1934, there were only seven of them on the seven daily papers, but they were now the final word for success or failure. And since they made their judgments on opening nights, it became increasingly important to producers to perfect their productions before these seven men got to see them. That is a major reason why tryouts became so important, and since Boston had seven theaters, one reason why Boston became important in the late twenties and during the thirties and ever since as one of the

places where all new plays and musicals must be tested.

Although there was no rigid pattern, producers began to send new shows first to New Haven for three days and nights, then, after a weekend which might be devoted to cutting and rewriting, to Boston, or Philadelphia, or to both cities for two full weeks "prior to Broadway." In some cases, the shows that came here under this system—and still do come, though in far fewer numbers—were close to final form; they were good for Boston playgoers and for the theater in Boston as an institution. Others, unfortunately, were not yet ready to be exhibited: in more than one instance, they opened and closed here because they were not only imperfect, but unperfectible. In 1940, by way of example, Tennessee Williams's first produced drama, "Battle of Angels," opened and closed at the Wilbur Theater, and the projected New York engagement was canceled. In 1975, "The Red Devil Battery Sign," by the same author, ceased to exist after only two weeks at the Shubert Theater. In the meantime, many others had been similarly presented and closed.

That these tryouts have provided Boston playgoers with much good entertainment during the last forty years is a fact. That the failures and the inadequacies of many of the newly tested shows have driven playgoers out of the theater forever is also true, and unfortunate. That we have come to depend on tryouts is true too; and "pity 't is 'tis true," for the number of those now available has been shrinking year after year.

The advantage of the tryout system is that it can and sometimes does offer Bostonians great shows in all their early freshness before the actors become bored or careless. The other side of the picture is that there have been in the past too many that were not ready. Showmen like Richard Rodgers and Oscar Hammerstein II took pains during their partnership not only to bring all their new musicals to Boston; they made sure that what they presented was, if imperfect, still generally worthwhile. Other producers, for whatever reasons, have not been so generous—or so wise. And Bostonians who have

seen two or three of these in a row, and sometimes have later learned that what they saw was only a rough version of what had since been perfected, have not been happy about it.

For many years, those who were unhappy about the abuses of the system could do little about it. Then the jets began to fly and the travel agencies began to offer excursions to New York with tickets to two or three hits that had already passed through their testing period and had been perfected, and it became possible for Bostonians to bypass the tryouts altogether and to do their playgoing in New York. That is what some of them still do.

In 1934, the seven commercial theaters of Boston were all owned or operated by the Shubert organization; most of them played new shows in tryout for New York, and little else. Twenty-two years later, when the Department of Justice filed suit against them for alleged monopoly, the Shuberts agreed to divest themselves of two playhouses here, then swiftly got rid of all but one. And although some Bostonians protested because one of those sold to be demolished was the Boston Opera House, there was very little fuss when the Plymouth, the Majestic, and the Copley were turned over to movie exhibitors and so taken out of of the live theater altogether.

For those who remained loyal and those who were still vitally interested in getting to see the new shows before they got to Broadway, the number of opportunities began to decrease after 1962, when Edward Albee's producers discovered they didn't have enough money to test "Who's Afraid of Virginia Woolf?" in New Haven and Boston, and decided instead to try that play out in a series of paid previews in New York as a substitute. "Who's Afraid of Virginia Woolf?" became, of course, a great popular success, and immediately producers with short bankrolls decided that they, too, might substitute previews in New York for tryouts in

Boston. By that time, the cost of producing plays had risen enormously and so had the expense of bringing to Boston and housing actors, scene designers, lighting artists, and all the others deemed necessary for proper play testing, not to mention the expense of transporting scenery, costumes, and properties.

There are other reasons why the number of new plays presented in Boston has diminished in the last ten years. One is the Kennedy Center for the Performing Arts in Washington, D. C., which contains in its marble halls a concert hall, a playhouse, and one opera house suitable for musical

*The drawings show Helen Hayes in a wheelchair as the old Queen Victoria at her Golden Jubilee and, inset, as the young Victoria.*

*"South Pacific" had its world premiere in New Haven, but of course had to be brought to Boston for judgment by the most perceptive audience in America.*

comedies and even for occasional plays whose casts are headed by stars of great popular renown: Ingrid Bergman, for example. Although it has been held in low regard architecturally ever since a critic of the New York *Times* deplored its white exterior, the Kennedy Center has been a tourist attraction of undoubted popularity since it opened in 1971, and a triumphant center for new plays and musical shows in tryout, competing with Boston and time and again putting on productions which previously would have played here.

The Kennedy Center was built with public funds and private contributions, but its managers depend on the sale of tickets to keep it going, and that means getting enough attractions to fill not only the Eisenhower Theater, which is for plays, but also the opera house and the large concert hall. That requires a great deal of planning and the expenditure of lots of money, privately raised. Fortunately, Roger L. Stevens, the operating director of the complex, is a courageous showman with a record of many shows on Broadway, and what is even nicer, he is rich and has rich friends. As producer, he knows how and where to find attractions that will grace, or in any case fill the center fifty-two weeks a year. And when there is a problem of raising funds, he is ingenious in solving it. More than once, when New York showmen have needed money to complete the capitalization of a new drama, he has supplied it. In return, the producers have been happy to play the Kennedy Center rather than Boston or Philadelphia; you can see their point.

He and his associates have offered other inducements that Boston theater managers have not been able to meet. The creators of one new comedy not only received investment money they needed from the Kennedy Center, but were also given, as a bonus in return for a four-weeks engagement, the entire scenic production, which was built for them at the Eisenhower Theater.

The producer of that particular entertainment,

opposite: *Joyous Mary Martin in the original production of "South Pacific" at the Shubert Theater in Boston.*

*Katharine Hepburn as Beatrice in "Much Ado About Nothing," one of her Shakespearean adventures on the stage in Boston.*

which subsequently became a popular New York hit, had wanted to play Boston for practical reasons. In his opinion, and that of others, tryouts in the Kennedy Center, while profitable, are unsettling because the audiences are by and large new to playgoing and therefore tend to be undiscriminating: they like almost everything. Boston audiences, being knowledgeable, are much more likely to react as New Yorkers will. And that, for nervous producers, authors, and directors trying desperately to discover in advance how the New York *Times* will react to their shows, is a matter of concern.

Even before the Kennedy Center opened, other cities had begun to compete for the new plays that for twenty-five years had almost always played Boston. For a few years it was Detroit, where a newly restored movie theater, the Fisher, offered

*Ethel Merman, a favorite in Boston season after season, in "Call Me Madam" at the Shubert Theater, 1950.*

large seating capacity and a big subscription audience. Los Angeles and San Francisco also developed huge subscription lists and so were able to guarantee the makers of new musicals up to fourteen weeks of large audiences, in addition to facilities for building scenery. Although it costs a lot to transport the players and the necessary equipment from New York to the West Coast, the journey can be arranged.

The managers of the Chandler Pavilion in Los Angeles need attractions to fill their three thousand seats, and like the operators of the Kennedy Center are willing and able to help finance the shows they originate. At this time, when it costs up to $1 million to get a musical show on and as much as $100,000 a week to keep it running, that sort of assistance is not only welcome, it is almost obligatory. And there are ways of bringing such a show back to New York from the Coast with intermediate playing dates, as David Merrick learned in October 1974 when he took Robert Preston and Bernadette Peters home from fourteen weeks of "Mack and Mabel" on the West Coast by way of the Dallas State Fair and the St. Louis Municipal Opera Theaters. Ten years earlier, Mr. Merrick

would have booked "Mack and Mabel" into New Haven and Boston and there would have learned from our alert audiences that more work was needed to make his show good enough for Broadway.

For a few years, Toronto proved attractive to playmakers with tryouts, especially those who were nurturing expensive musicals. For the O'Keefe Center in that bustling, hustling city seats three thousand people, and that is nearly twice as many as our Shubert or Colonial. But Rodgers and Hammerstein discovered and warned Alan Jay Lerner and Frederick Loewe that jumping from the O'Keefe directly into such comparatively small playhouses as the New York Winter Garden was unwise: better to break the jump by stopping off here at the Colonial. So the O'Keefe helped rather than hurt, because shows that were introduced

there, as for example the Richard Burton "Hamlet," had some, though not all, of their rough edges smoothed before Boston.

These competing cities and such others as Baltimore, which became important in 1976-1977 as a new tryout center, each had its own advantages that Boston couldn't match, and all had and still have in common great lists of theater subscribers: playgoers so eager to see new attractions and so well-heeled that they buy tickets in advance of the season for anywhere from six to eight productions, thus guaranteeing nervous producers that whatever the quality of their new work, they will have a respectably large audience and a considerable amount of money in the box office to insure against total losses. For thirty years, Boston had a large subscription audience, too, created by the Theater Guild of New York and maintained by the collateral American Theater Society. Since 1970, that audience has dwindled down to a precious few and in dwindling has made it risky for showmen to bring in those attractions that have been costly and unconventional; it has sometimes been safer to take such shows to Washington or Baltimore or Toronto, or even the Los Angeles-San Francisco circuit.

*The Royal Shakespeare Company celebrated the 400th anniversary of Shakespeare's birth by presenting two of his greatest works, "King Lear" and "The Comedy of Errors," at the Shubert in Boston in 1964. The picture shows the first scene of "King Lear," with Paul Scofield as the old king railing at Diana Rigg as his stubborn daughter, Cordelia.*

The Theater Guild subscription list shrank from twenty thousand Bostonians to one third of that formidable number for many reasons. The Guild began in New York in 1919 as an adventurous team of producers putting on the more advanced European dramatists and then the major plays of Shaw, O'Neill, S. N. Behrman, and others, and later such innovative musicals as "Oklahoma!" and "Carousel." They first created a subscription audience in New York to support their shows, then extended it to other cities, and in the beginning sent out six plays, all of which they originated and most of which had some distinct merits. But the costs of production became so great that they had to go to other managers for some of their shows. Then, when Lawrence Langner and Teresa Helburn, their longest-surviving directors, passed on, they began to rely more and more on people whose interests were different, and, in some cases, on producers who insisted they, the Guild, take risky shows along with those that were established in order to fill their lists.

In Boston during the late twenties and thirties, the Guild's first-night list was made up to a large extent of the same proper ladies and gentlemen who had tickets for the Friday Symphony and the opening night of the Metropolitan Opera; some families passed them down from one generation to the next. But as the Guild began to send in plays that were notably imperfect, and others that espoused the new permissiveness, older subscribers began to protest; others simply dropped out. (In cultivated Bostonians over thirty, there is as there always has been a surviving strain of puritanism. Their juniors reject, deplore, and deride this. But juniors don't buy subscriptions to anything; they are hitgoers, not supporters of the arts.)

In 1940, senior Guildgoers protested so vehemently against the lurid aspects of Tennessee Williams's, "Battle of Angels," that the Guild closed it at the Wilbur. Some subscribers canceled at that time, and although a few came back seven years later for his "A Streetcar Named Desire" in the same theater, their faith had been shaken.

Later, in 1956, some of them walked—no, say, rather, stalked—out of Harold Pinter's "The Homecoming." More recently Simon Gray's "Otherwise Engaged" turned off at least a few.

On May 12, 1977, the whole Theatre Guild-American Theater Society subscription system crumbled and quietly expired after forty-nine years of serving Boston's playgoers, bringing in plays and sometimes musicals that were often unusual, sometimes rather extraordinary, and, in the beginning at least, had already been tested and finalized. The end came with an abrupt announcement by the Shubert Organization that it had established its own subscription system, offering six plays during the season of 1977-1978 to subscribers, at the Shubert Theater only.

The Shubert Organization dates back to 1900 when Lee, J. J., and Sam S. Shubert, three shrewd young men of Syracuse, began to buy up theaters in New York. It consists now of four corporations and the nonprofit Shubert Foundation, with assets estimated at $100 million and ownership of theaters from coast to coast. The power of the organization is great and, under a new administration created three years ago, prudently administered. Because of it, the Shuberts will be able to deliver to their Boston subscribers the shows they are now offering. They have a large investment in "A Chorus Line" and in other hits, and they own most of the theaters that producers must get on Broadway. When they say "A Chorus Line," or any other production, will be delivered to subscribers at their theater, we can count on it. One of the problems of the Guild subscription system since 1960 was that its managers were forced too often to announce shows that for one reason or another never got here.

Our other commercial theaters, the Colonial and the Wilbur—the first owned by and the second under lease to the Jujamcyn Corporation, have also developed their own solutions to the subscription problem.

Two weeks before the Shuberts put the Theater Guild subscription list out of business, Jujamcyn announced the retirement of Samuel H. Schwartz,

who had been sole operating trustee of their playhouses, and in that capacity had made several ingenious and useful moves to improve the quality of theater in Boston. Instead of booking none but the available tryouts into the Wilbur, he brought into that playhouse established shows which had been perfected elsewhere in productions that were in all ways first-rate. Through his foresight and because of his willingness to run financial risks, Bostonians got to see in extended engagements and with excellent casts "You're a Good Man, Charlie Brown," "Hair," "Godspell," "The Boys in the Band," "No Place to Be Somebody," and in 1976, in the longest continuous engagement of any straight play, the English melodrama "Equus," which ran for seven months.

A new man, Richard G. Wolff, took over from Mr. Schwartz. It is his obligation to create for his two theaters their own subscription series to meet the competition of the Shubert plan.

Since 1956, when the Shuberts yielded the Colonial and Wilbur theaters to the Jujamcyn Group and abandoned to wreckers or movie companies the Opera House, the Copley, the Plymouth, and the Majestic, Boston has supported its three commercial theaters with considerable fidelity despite the decreasing number and sometimes unsatisfactory quality of new shows, the weakness of the Theatre Guild, and for several years the physical decline of the theater district. Although musicals continue to be favored here, as they are in other cities, most plays of reasonable merit, and many others which can be considered controversial—as, for example, Simon Gray's "Otherwise Engaged" and Tom Stoppard's dramaturgic antic, "Travesties"—have been successful. An audience is still there for these Broadway shows, as it has been since the Colonial opened seventy-seven years ago, and although the numbers are smaller than they

opposite: *When Tallulah Bankhead opened here in Cocteau's "Eagle Rampant" at the Plymouth Theater in 1946, young Marlon Brando was in the cast, but not for long. He was fired during the first week by Tallulah.*

JOHN C. WILSON

*presents*

# TALLULAH
# BANKHEAD

*in*

## "EAGLE RAMPANT"

By JEAN COCTEAU

(Adapted from the French by RONALD DUNCAN)

*with*

**MARLON
BRANDO** · **CLARENCE
DERWENT** · **COLIN
KEITH-JOHNSTON**

*Settings by*
**DONALD OENSLAGER**

*Costumes by*
**ALINE BERNSTEIN**

*Staged by* **MR. WILSON**

# PLYMOUTH THEATRE
BOSTON
## 2 Weeks Only, Beg. Monday, December 9
MATINEES THURSDAY and SATURDAY

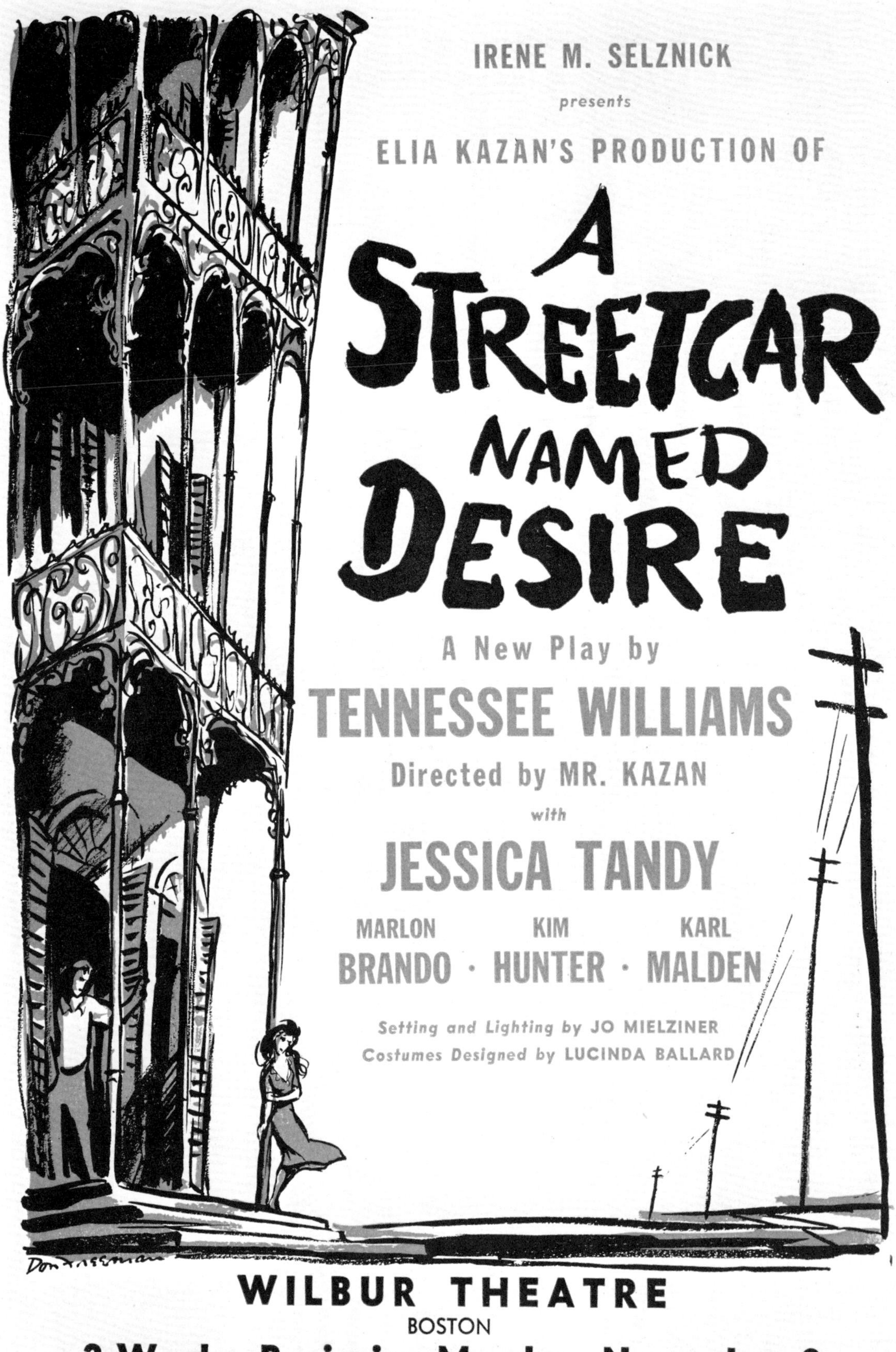

IRENE M. SELZNICK

*presents*

ELIA KAZAN'S PRODUCTION OF

# A STREETCAR NAMED DESIRE

A New Play by

## TENNESSEE WILLIAMS

Directed by MR. KAZAN

*with*

## JESSICA TANDY

MARLON · KIM · KARL
BRANDO · HUNTER · MALDEN

*Setting and Lighting by* JO MIELZINER
*Costumes Designed by* LUCINDA BALLARD

## WILBUR THEATRE
BOSTON
### 2 Weeks, Beginning Monday, November 3
MATINEES WEDNESDAY and SATURDAY

*Jessica Tandy and Marlon Brando in the original production of "A Streetcar Named Desire" at the Wilbur Theater in Boston in 1947. It was his performance as Stanley Kowalski that projected him into stardom. Miss Tandy was the original Blanche Dubois.*

once were, the general alertness and perceptiveness is rather high.

In addition to these commercial theaters, we have the Charles which, since 1970, when it ceased to operate as a regional theater, has been run with some success as a booking house for Off Broadway productions, and the new Boston Repertory Theater.

Three commercial theaters, one Off Broadway house, and one that comes closer to the Off Off Broadway style are not so many in a city that once had thirteen playhouses. In view of the competition, however, the easy allure of television, and perhaps the dinner theaters—though most of their patrons seem to be new showgoers—it is not bad. And this nucleus is supplemented by a variety of theaters on the fringe of downtown, with others just beginning or organizing; the ambition to create a fully professional resident theater here has never died.

There are three little theaters not far from the center of town, each with a more or less precarious hold on its own audience. Since 1975, the Boston Shakespeare Company has been putting on the dramas of the master with a mixture of professional and amateur competence and has now acquired a commodious playhouse in Horticultural Hall. In the old theater over the fish market where the Charles Playhouse Company began, an organization known as the Lyric Theater presents dramas of established quality, from Ibsen to Williams. The playhouse that the new little theater

*Recognize him? Laurence Olivier, now a lord and our greatest living actor, in his favorite role: as the third-rate ham, Archie Rice, in John Osborne's drama, "The Entertainer," which he introduced to America at the Shubert in Boston.*

*Jason Robards, Jr., as Macbeth, in a production presented by the Cambridge Drama Festival at the Metropolitan Boston Arts Center in August 1959. Siobhan McKenna was Lady Macbeth. This one did not get to New York.*

**BROCK PEMBERTON**

*presents*

# FRANK FAY

*in*

# "THE POOKA"

*A New Comedy by* MARY CHASE

*with*

# JOSEPHINE HULL

*Directed by* **ANTOINETTE PERRY**

*Settings by* **JOHN ROOT**

●

## COPLEY THEATRE

COPLEY SQUARE, BOSTON

### 2 Weeks Only Com. Tues., Oct. 17

MATINEES THURSDAY AND SATURDAY

---

# SAM S. SHUBERT THEATRE

SHUBERT HOLDING CO., Proprietors and Managers
A. G. MUNRO, Resident Manager

---

GILBERT MILLER and LESLIE HOWARD
In Association with ARTHUR HOPKINS

Present

LESLIE HOWARD

in

## "THE PETRIFIED FOREST"

A Play in Two Acts

by

ROBERT E. SHERWOOD

Staged by ARTHUR HOPKINS
Setting by RAYMOND SOVEY

CAST
(In the Order of Appearance)

| | |
|---|---|
| A TELEGRAPHER | Milo Boulton |
| ANOTHER TELEGRAPHER | James Doody |
| BOZE HERTZLINGER | Frank Milan |
| JASON MAPLE | Walter Vonnegut |
| PAULA | Esther Leeming |
| GRAMP MAPLE | Charles Dow Clark |
| GABBY MAPLE | Peggy Conklin |
| ALAN SQUIER | Leslie Howard |
| HERB | Robert Porterfield |
| MRS. CHISHOLM | Blanche Sweet |
| MR. CHISHOLM | Robert Hudson |
| JOSEPH | John Alexander |
| JACKIE | Ross Hertz |
| RUBY | Tom Fadden |
| DUKE MANTEE | Humphrey Bogart |
| PYLES | Slim Thompson |
| COMMANDER KLEPP | Aloysius Cunningham |
| HENDY | Guy Conradi |
| SHERIFF | Frank Tweddell |
| A DEPUTY | Eugene Keith |
| ANOTHER DEPUTY | Harry Sherwin |

The scene is the Black Mesa Bar-B-Q, a gas station and lunch room at a lonely crossroads in the eastern Arizona desert.

The action begins late in the afternoon of an autumn day in the present year and continues into the evening of the same day.

| | |
|---|---|
| Frank Perley | Company Manager |
| Helen Deutsch | Press Representative |
| Edward McHugh | Stage Manager |

---

*A surprise hit of the 1944 season at the Copley Theater, "The Pooka" by Mary Coyle Chase starring Frank Fay, had its name changed during the Boston tryout to "Harvey."*

*A historic playbill: when "The Petrified Forest" by Robert E. Sherwood opened its pre-Broadway tour at the Shubert in Boston in 1936, Leslie Howard was starred. The name of the actor who played "Duke Mantee" was in small type; Humphrey Bogart hadn't been discovered yet.*

---

company called the Next Move opened at 955 Boylston Street, opposite the Prudential Center, is a converted stable, used once by the mounted police.

There are two small continuing theaters in Cambridge, the Caravan and the Cambridge Ensemble, both in church halls. The first is dedicated largely to original plays that reflect the feelings prevalent

in the women's liberation movement. The Cambridge Ensemble, whose actors split off from the Caravan in 1973, presents its audiences with some new plays and some modern and ancient classics.

The total capacity of all the "fringe theaters" and of three makeshift playhouses in the basement of the Boston Center for the Arts at 551 Tremont

Street is far less than that of the Wilbur Theater. Audiences are small, but in some cases devoted; some are composed of college or high-school students who like the lower ticket prices and admire the special points of view of the producers. The Little Flags Collective, for example, which has been more or less hidden in one of the basements of the Boston Center for the Arts, has been putting on dramas of the political Left since 1976.

More ambitious is the Massachusetts Center Repertory Theater, which was organized as a professional resident company and after one failure in 1975, emerged in the spring of 1977 with three plays featuring imported stars at the Shubert Theater; its future is not clear at this time.

*Roddy MacDowall and Richard Burton in the musical "Camelot."*

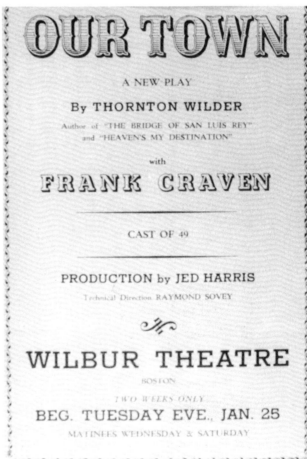

*Playbill for the premiere here of Thornton Wilder's "Our Town," at the Wilbur Theater in 1938. It went on to New York to become a beloved American classic.*

*Alfred Lunt and Lynn Fontanne, the American theater's greatest acting team of the twentieth century, shown in "The Visit," in 1956, at the Shubert Theater, opening the American tour of their last play.*

*Paul Robeson in "Othello" with Uta Hagen as Desdemona at the Cambridge Summer Theater in Brattle Hall, Cambridge, in the summer of 1942, in the premiere of the first American production ever to present an actor of his race as the Moor of Venice.*

*John Wood, the great English actor, had a personal triumph at the Colonial Theater in 1977 in Tom Stoppard's "Travesties."*

As this is written, it is evident that an opportunity exists for a new resident repertory company, to be developed and maintained on the highest level of professional excellence, to take over, perhaps, the Wilbur Theater, to give Boston its own center of great drama, greatly acted. We had such companies before. Now is the time of challenge.

# EPILOGUE

In June of '78, a spokesman for Jujamcyn Theaters announced that his company will drop its lease on the Wilbur Theater on August 1, 1979. There were no immediate bidders to take over the playhouse and although a representative declared that the New England Medical Center, the owner, would like to see it used as a public theater, he intimated that prospective operators had better come forward soon: the Center needs space for a lecture hall, and the Wilbur could be it.

This ominous announcement came ironically at a time when the City of Boston was deeply involved in new activity to upgrade the theater district. Mayor Kevin H. White had committed substantial funds to plant trees and construct new pavements and had invited Benjamin Thompson, the architect of the Faneuil Hall restoration, to prepare a plan which would tie the section together as a handsome urban unit.

Even as Ben Thompson began the first discussions, however, there were rumblings from New York that suggested he could be creating a frame for a depleted, or diminished, theater.

The producer of a new Broadway musical called, appropriately, "A Broadway Musical," announced that instead of testing his show in Boston, as he had originally planned, he would open it as a "workshop" in a New York church hall. Explaining, one of his associates said: "We must find new ways to get our shows on."

Commenting on this new way of trying out shows that would have gone to Boston or Philadelphia in the past, John Corry wrote in the New York Times: "It is expensive to open in Philadelphia, say, and then bomb in Boston. It is expensive in Boston. It is better you should bomb somewhere else."

To "bomb" in Boston during the kind of test run that has filled most of our theaters down through the past fifty years costs a great deal more in money than to put a new show together in the Riverside Church; it is less costly, too, in prestige.

To fail in the church would mean no more than closing down a "workshop." To open and close in Los Angeles, at the Music Center, would not be inexpensive, but the failure would resound far less loudly in New York, which is the center of things. There are now many other "new ways to get shows on" without the risk of bombing in Boston. The producers of the award-winning revue "Ain't Misbehavin'" tried it out in a cafe theater Off Off Broadway. Instead of a Boston engagement, with high costs of trucking and union wages for setting it up and taking it down and then the possibility of closing disastrously, Elizabeth Swados prepared her "Runaways" for Broadway under the protection of Joseph Papp in his New York Public Theater where experimentation is the name of the game and failure serves only to make room for the next project.

Jerome Lawrence and Robert E. Lee opened their newest play, "First Monday in October" in Washington during the spring of 1978. With the Kennedy Center's huge subscription list and with Henry Fonda as star, they had guarantees against financial loss. And if in ten advertised weeks they should not be able to improve text and performances sufficiently, they might safely have closed it down. To close at the Kennedy Center, where many productions play exclusive engagements, is not a catastrophe. To open a show there, to revise and rewrite it and then, having avoided Boston altogether, take it to New York, is reasonable, too: the producers and authors of "First Mon-

day in October" have done just that, leaving Boston with one less show for theaters like the Wilbur.

Jujamcyn is abandoning the Wilbur because there are too few new shows now to take advantage of its comforts and its intimacy, and too many "other ways to get our shows on" for timid producers.

So now, as of August 15, 1978, the future of the Wilbur is doubtful and Boston's entire focus as a tryout center—Broadway down East—is changing.

The productions coming into the Colonial and Shubert are mostly road companies of established Broadway successes, and there will be fewer and fewer of these.

Out of this changing situation, one hopes, Boston may be able to get a good resident theater company, based, perhaps, at the Wilbur Theater. A really first rate company this time, managed by great professionals, with adequate resources to sustain occasional failure.

# APPENDIX A
## PRINCIPAL THEATERS FROM 1792

## a. Theaters Listed in Alphabetical Order

B. F. Keith's Theater (1894-1952)
Boston Museum (1841-1846)
Boston Museum (1846-1903)
Boston Opera House (1909-1957)
Boston Repertory Theater (1976-    )
Boston Theater (also called Federal Street Theater)
  (1794-1852)
Boston Theater (1854-1925)
Bowdoin Square Theater (1892-1955)

Castle Square Theater (1894-1932)
Charles Playhouse (1947-    )
Chickering Hall (1901-1975)
Colonial Theater (1900-    )
Columbia Theater (1891-1955)
Continental Theater (1866-1873)
Copley Theater (1916-1957)
Cort Theater (1914-1915)

Globe Theater (1870-1873)
Globe Theater (1874-1903)
Globe Theater (1903-    )
Grand Opera House (1888-1956)

Haymarket Theater (1796-1803)
Hollis Street Theater (1885-1935)
Howard Athenaeum (1845-1953)

Lion Theater (1836-1878)

Majestic Theater (1903-    )
Metropolitan Theater (1925-    )

National Theater (1832-1863)
National Theater (1911-    )
New Exhibition Room (1792-1793)
Next Move Theater (1977-    )

Park Theater (1879-    )
Plymouth Theater (1911-    )

Repertory Theater of Boston (1925-1939)

Selwyn's Theater (1867-1870)
Shubert Theater (1910-    )

Toy Theater (1911-1913)
Toy Theater (1914-1916)
Tremont Theater (1827-1843)
Tremont Theater (1889-1949)

Wilbur Theater (1914-    )
Windsor Theater (1882-1888)

## b. Theaters Listed Alphabetically by Street

BOWDOIN STREET

21. *Bowdoin Square Theater* (1 Bowdoin St.)
February 15, 1892 - May 27, 1955
West End

BOYLSTON PLACE

40. *Boston Repertory Theater* (1 Boylston Pl.)
1976 -
Made from Ace Recording Studio

BOYLSTON STREET

24. *Colonial Theater* (100 Boylston St.)
1900 -

Next Move Theater (955 Boylston St.)
1977 -
Opposite Prudential Center

CHARLES STREET

9. *Charles Playhouse* (54 Charles St.)
1957 -
Moved to 74 Warrenton Street in the following
year

DARTMOUTH STREET

35. *Toy Theater*
1914 - 1916
Opposite Copley Plaza. Became Copley Theater, 1916, moved to Stuart Street, 1922

FEDERAL STREET

2. *Boston Theater*
February 3, 1794 - May 8, 1852
Also called Federal Street Theater. Corner
Franklin. Burned down 1798, rebuilt. Also
known as Odeon (1835), used as lecture hall
several years, reopened 1846 as a playhouse

HAWLEY STREET

1. *New Exhibition Room*
August 10, 1792 - 1793
Hawley Street was originally "Board Alley"

HOLLIS STREET

17. *Hollis Street Theater*
1885 - 1935
Near Tremont, where parking garage is now,
opposite Shubert

HOWARD STREET

8. *Howard Athenaeum*
October 13, 1845 - 1953
On Howard Street near present State Office
Building, in the West End. Former Millerite
temple. Second (after fire) on same site
opened July 4, 1846

HUNTINGTON AVENUE

28. *Boston Opera House* (343 Huntington Ave.)
November 9, 1909 - September 25, 1957

37. *Repertory Theater of Boston* (264 Huntington
Avenue)
Opposite Symphony Hall. Closed 1939, be-
came Esquire Movie Theater. Later, name
changed to Civic Repertory Theater. Became
Boston University Theater in 1958

25. *Chickering Hall*
1901 - 1975
Near Massachusetts Ave. Became St. James
Theater, 1912; later, Uptown Movie

LIME STREET

32. *Toy Theater*
1911 - 1913
Foot of Beacon Hill

PARK SQUARE

33. *Cort Theater*
January 19, 1914 - May 29, 1915
Later called Selwyn (no connection with earlier
Selwyn's Theater)

PORTLAND STREET

5. *National Theater*
February 27, 1832 - March 24, 1863
Opened as American Amphitheater, changed
to Warren Theater same year. Name changed
to National in 1836. Later called People's
National Union Concert Hall, etc.

STUART STREET

36. *Copley Theater*
1922 - ca. 1971
Toy Theater turned around, amplified, moved
to Stuart Street. Became Capri moviehouse,
1957

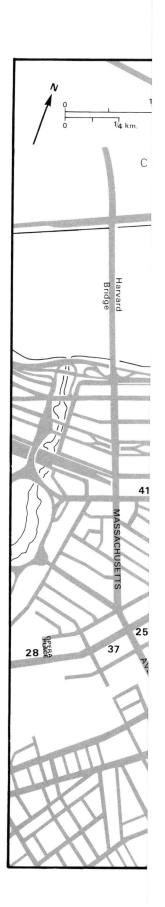

N

0       1

0     1/4 km.

C

Harvard
Bridge

41

MASSACHUSETTS

25

OPERA
PLACE

28    37

A

30. *Plymouth Theater*
    1911-     (131 Stuart Street)
    Near Tremont. Became Gary movie theater, 1958

TREMONT STREET

7. *Boston Museum*
   June 14, 1841-1846
   Tremont at Bromfield. As Boston Museum and Gallery of Fine Arts, upper hall used for concerts, variety. In February 1843, hall became dramatic theater

9. *Boston Museum*
   November 2, 1846-1903
   New building Tremont St., adjacent to King's Chapel burying ground

22. *Castle Square Theater*
    Corner Chandler, South End. Name changed to Arlington in 1919, then back to original name. Closed in 1927; razed in 1932

3. *Haymarket Theater*
   December 26, 1796-March 1803
   Near Boylston, opposite Common

26. *Majestic Theater* (219 Tremont St.)
    1903-
    Became Saxon movie theater, 1958

29. *Shubert Theater* (265 Tremont St.)
    1910-

TREMONT STREET, continued

4. *Tremont Theater*
   September 24, 1827-June 23, 1843
   Originally Common Street, where Tremont Temple now stands

19. *Tremont Theater*
    1889-     (176 Tremont St. at Avery)
    Remodeled and renamed Astor Theater, 1949

34. *Wilbur Theater*
    1914-     (252 Tremont St., near corner Stuart)

WASHINGTON STREET

23. *B. F. Keith's Theater*
    1894-1952
    Between Avery and West, next to Boston Theater. Closed in 1928, became Shubert Apollo Theater, 1929-30. Name changed to Shubert Lyric Theater, 1930-34 (these both legitimate theaters). Became moviehouse, Normandie, then Laff Movie

10. *Boston Theater*
    September 11, 1854-1925
    Name changed to Boston Academy of Music, 1860-62, between Avery and West. Became Keith Boston, 1914. (In 1925 a new Keith Boston, also called RKO Boston, opened across Washington St., at Essex. This later became Cinerama, then Essex)

20. *Columbia Theater* (978 Washington St.)
    1891-1955
    South End, near corner of present Herald St.

11. *Continental Theater*
    January 1, 1866-1873
    Corner Harvard Street, South End

13. *Globe Theater*
    September 12, 1870-1873
    Was Selwyn's renamed, and opened under new management

14. *Globe Theater*
    1874-1903
    Between Boylston and Kneeland

27. *Globe Theater*
    1903-
    Corner Kneeland. Became Center Theater movie

6. *Lion Theater*
   January 11, 1836-1878
   Between Avery and West. Became Melodeon Theater, 1839; Gaiety Theater, 1878

15. *Park Theater*
    April 14, 1879-
    Near corner Boylston. Became Minsky's Park Burlesque, 1930; then Trans-Lux, then State Theater

12. *Selwyn's Theater*
    October 29, 1867-1870
    Between Essex and Hayward Place. Became Globe Theater, September 12, 1870

16. *Windsor Theater*
    ca. 1880-May 30, 1888
    Near Dover. Became Grand Dime Museum, 1886; New Grand Theater, 1896

## c. Theaters Listed Chronologically

| Opened | Theater | Closed |
|---|---|---|
| 1 August 10, 1792 | *New Exhibition Room*<br>Board Alley, now Hawley St.; ran two seasons. | 1793 |
| 2 February 3, 1794 | *Boston Theater*<br>Also called Federal St. Theater. Federal St. at the corner of Franklin. Burned down 1798; rebuilt. Also known as Odeon (1835); used as lecture hall for several years, reopened in 1846 as a playhouse. | May 8, 1852 |
| 3 December 26, 1796 | *Haymarket Theater*<br>Tremont St. near Boylston, opposite Common. | March 1803 |
| 4 September 24, 1827 | *Tremont Theater*<br>Tremont, then Common St., where Tremont Temple now stands. | June 23, 1843 |
| 5 February 27, 1832 | *National Theater*<br>Portland St. Opened as American Amphitheater, changed to Warren Theater same year. Name changed to National, 1836. Later called People's National Union Concert Hall, etc. | March 24, 1863 |
| 6 January 11, 1836 | *Lion Theater*<br>Washington St., between Avery and West. Became Melodeon Theater, 1839; Gaiety Theater, 1878. | 1878 |
| 7 June 14, 1841 | *Boston Museum*<br>Tremont at Bromfield. As Boston Museum and Gallery of Fine Arts, upper hall used for concerts, variety. In February 1843, hall became dramatic theater. | 1846 |
| 8 October 13, 1845 | *Howard Athenaeum*<br>Howard St., near present State Office Building in West End. Former Millerite temple. Second (after fire) on same site opened July 4, 1846. | 1953 [Razed 1962] |
| 9 November 2, 1846 | *Boston Museum*<br>New building Tremont St., adjacent to King's Chapel burying ground. | 1903 |
| 10 September 11, 1854 | *Boston Theater*<br>Washington St. between Avery and West. Name changed to Boston Academy of Music, 1860-1862. Became Keith Boston, 1914. (In 1925, a new Keith Boston, also called RKO Boston, opened across Washington St. at Essex. This later became Cinerama, then Essex.) | 1925 |

11  January 1, 1866      *Continental Theater*      1873
Washington St. at Harvard, South End.

12  October 29, 1867      *Selwyn's Theater*      1870
Washington St., between Essex and Hayward Place. Became Globe Theater, September 12, 1870.

13  September 12, 1870      *Globe Theater*      1873
Was Selwyn's renamed, and opened under new management.

14  1874      *Globe Theater*      1903
Washington St., between Boylston and Kneeland.

15  April 14, 1879      *Park Theater*
Washington St., near the corner of Boylston. Became Minsky's Park Burlesque, 1930; then Trans-Lux, then State Theater.

16  October 16, 1882      *Windsor Theater*      May 30, 1888
Corner of Washington St. at Dover. Became Grand Dime Museum, 1886; New Grand Theater, 1896.

17  November 9, 1885      *Hollis Street Theater*      1935
On Hollis St. near Tremont, where parking garage is now; opposite Shubert.

18  July 2, 1888      *Grand Opera House*
Washington St. near Dover.

19  1889      *Tremont Theater*
176 Tremont St., at Avery. Remodeled and renamed Astor Theater, 1949.

20  1891      *Columbia Theater*      1955
978 Washington St. in the South End, near present Herald St. Moviehouse after 1915.

21  February 15, 1892      *Bowdoin Square Theater*      May 27, 1955
One Bowdoin St. in the West End.

22  1894      *Castle Square Theater*      1932
Tremont St. at the corner of Chandler, in the South End. Name changed to Arlington, 1919, then back to original name. Closed in 1927, razed in 1932.

23  1894      *B. F. Keith's Theater*      1952
Washington St. between Avery and West, next to Boston Theater. Closed in 1928, became Shubert Apollo Theater, 1929-1930; changed

to Shubert Lyric Theater, 1930-1934 (these both legitimate theaters). Then moviehouse, Normandie, then Laff Movie.

24 December 20, 1900      *Colonial Theater*
100 Boylston Street.

25 1901      *Chickering Hall*      1975
Huntington Ave., near Mass. Ave. Became St. James Theater, 1912; later, Uptown movie.

26 February 16, 1903      *Majestic Theater*
219 Tremont St. Became moviehouse, Saxon, 1958.

27 1903      *Globe Theater*
Washington St. at the corner of Kneeland. Became Center Theater, movie.

28 November 9, 1909      *Boston Opera House*      September 25, 1957
343 Huntington Ave. in the Back Bay.

29 January 24, 1910      *Shubert Theater*
265 Tremont St.

30 September 23, 1911      *Plymouth Theater*
131 Stuart St., near Tremont. Became Gary movie theater, 1958.

31 1911      *National Theater*
551 Tremont, near Dover. First called Waldorf.

32 1911      *Toy Theater*      1913
Lime Street, at the foot of Beacon Hill.

33 January 19, 1914      *Cort Theater*      May 29, 1915
Park Square. Later called Selwyn. (No connection with earlier Selwyn's Theater.)

34 April 19, 1914      *Wilbur Theater*
252 Tremont St., near the corner of Stuart.

35 1914      *Toy Theater*      1922
Dartmouth St., opposite Copley Plaza. Became Copley Theater, 1916. Moved to Stuart St., 1922.

36 1916      *Copley Theater*      ca. 1971
Toy Theater renamed and, in 1922, moved to Stuart St. between Dartmouth and Huntington Ave. Became Capri moviehouse, 1957.

37 1925            *Repertory Theater of Boston*
264 Huntington Ave. opposite Symphony Hall. Closed 1930, became Esquire Movie Theater; later, name changed to Civic Repertory Theater. Became Boston University Theater in 1958.

38 1925            *Metropolitan Theater*
268 Tremont. Became Music Hall, 1958.

39 1957            *Charles Playhouse*
54 Charles St. near Beacon. Company moved to 74 Warrenton St. in the same year.

40 1976            *Boston Repertory Theater*
1 Boylston Place. Made from Ace Recording Studio.

41 1977            *Next Move Theater*
955 Boylston St., opposite Prudential Center.

# APPENDIX B
## SOME LONG RUNS IN BOSTON THEATERS

(Plays — P; Musicals — M)

| Opening Date | Production | Theater | Number of weeks |
|---|---|---|---|
| December 11, 1971 | "Godspell" (M) | Wilbur | 86 |
| November 16, 1972 | "One Flew Over the Cuckoo's Nest" (P) | Charles Playhouse | 72 |
| December 13, 1967 | "You're A Good Man, Charlie Brown" (M) | Wilbur | 49 |
| March 6, 1970 | "Hair" (M) | Wilbur | 40 |
| October 5, 1925 | "Abie's Irish Rose" (P) | Castle Square | 31 |
| June 1, 1976 | "Don't Bother Me, I Can't Cope" (M) | Charles Playhouse | 31 |
| November 18, 1975 | "Equus" (P) | Wilbur | 29 ½ |
| April 13, 1925 | "Rose-Marie" (M) | Shubert, then Majestic in one continuous run | 29 |
| December 22, 1913 | "Under Cover" (P)) | Plymouth | 27½ |
| January 3, 1910 | "The Man From Home" (P) | Park | 27 |
| February 8, 1892 | "1492" (M) | Park | 26 |
| September 3, 1891 | "The County Fair" (P) | Park | 26 |
| May 10, 1970 | "Jacques Brel Is Alive and Well . . . and Living in Paris" (M) | Charles Playhouse | 25 |
| September 30, 1940 | "Life with Father" (P) | Civic Repretory | 24 |
| December 5, 1892 | "Temperance Town" (P) | Park | 24 |
| September 4, 1922 | "The Bat" (P) | Wilbur | 24 |
| February 5, 1917 | "Fair and Warmer" (P) | Park Square | 23 |
| December 25, 1922 | "Lightnin'" (P) | Hollis | 21 |
| November 9, 1885 | "The Mikado" (M) | Hollis | 20 |
| September 17, 1914 | "Peg O' My Heart" (P) | Cort | 20 |
| December 23, 1912 | "Disraeli" (P) | Plymouth | 19 |
| May 4, 1925 | "No, No, Nanette" (M) | Tremont | 19 |
| May 10, 1920 | "Mary" (M) | Tremont | 19 |
| September 4, 1893 | "The Black Crook" (M) | Boston | 18 |

# SELECTIVE BIBLIOGRAPHY

Armstrong, Margaret. *Fanny Kemble, A Passionate Victorian.* New York: Macmillian, 1938.

Binns, Archie. *Mrs. Fiske and the American Theatre.* New York: Crown, 1955.

Boyer, Paul S. *Purity in Print.* New York: Scribner, 1968.

Clapp, William W., Jr. *A Record of the Boston Stage.* Boston: J. Munroe, 1853.

Crawford, Mary Caroline. *Romance of the American Theatre.* Boston: Little, Brown, 1913.

Dempsey, David and Raymond P. Baldwin. *Triumphs and Trials of Lotta Crabtree.* New York: Morrow, 1968.

Dunlap, William. *A History of the American Theatre.* New York: Harper, 1832.

Edgett, Edwin Francis. *I Speak for Myself.* New York: Macmillan, 1940.

Flanagan, Hallie. *Arena.* New York: Duell, Sloan and Pearce, 1940.

Fowler, Gene. *Good Night, Sweet Prince.* New York: Viking, 1944.

French, Charles Elwell. *Six Years of Drama at the Castle Square Theatre.* Boston: C. E. French, 1903.

Gelb, Arthur and Barbara. *O'Neill.* New York: Harper, 1962.

Hogan, Robert. *Dion Boucicault.* New York: Twayne, 1969.

Houseman, John. *Run-through; A Memoir.* New York: Simon and Schuster, 1972.

Hughes, Elinor. *Passing Through to Broadway.* Boston: Waverly House, 1948.

King, Donald C. "Historical Survey of the Theatre in Boston," *Marquee,* Journal of the Theatre Historical Society. VI: 3 (3rd quarter, 1974), pp. 6-22.

Kinne, Wisner. *George Pierce Baker and the American Theater.* Cambridge, Mass.: Harvard University Press, 1954.

Kotsilibas-Davis, James. *Great Times, Good Times: The Odyssey of Maurice Barrymore.* Garden City, N.Y.: Doubleday, 1977.

Krause, David. *Sean O'Casey and His World.* New York: Scribner, 1976.

Langner, Lawrence. *The Magic Curtain.* New York: Dutton, 1951.

Leach, Joseph. *Bright Particular Star, the Life and Times of Charlotte Cushman.* New Haven, Conn.: Yale University Press, 1970.

Leavitt, M. B. *Fifty Years in Theatrical Management.* New York: Broadway, 1912.

Lifson, Davis S. *Yiddish Theatre in America.* New York: T. Yoseloff, 1965.

McCaughey, Robert A. *Josiah Quincy, 1772-1864.* Cambridge, Mass.: Harvard University Press, 1974.

McCord, David. *H.T.P.: Portrait of a Critic.* New York: Coward-McCann, 1935.

McGlinchee, Claire. *First Decade of the Boston Museum*. Boston: B. Humphries, 1940.

McNamara, Brooks. *American Playhouses in the 18th Century*. Cambridge, Mass.: Harvard University Press, 1969.

Mates, Julian. *American Musical Stage Before 1800*. New Brunswick, N.J.: Rutgers University Press, 1962.

Moody, Richard, ed. *Dramas from the American Theatre, 1762-1909*. Cleveland: World, 1966.

Morehouse, Ward. "Famous American Theatres—the Castle Square," *Theatre Arts*, XLI: 8 August, 1957), pp. 30.

Nadel, Norman. *Pictorial History of the Theatre Guild*. New York: Crown, 1969.

Newhall, F. H. "The theatre; a discourse preached at the Bromfield Street M.E. Church, March 15, 1863." Boston: Magee, 1863.

Norton, Elliot. "Boston" chapter in *Best Plays of 1949-50, 50-51, 51-52, 61-62, 62-63, 63-64, 65-66, 66-67*, and "Theatre in New England" in *Best Plays of 1974-75*. New York: Dodd Mead.

_____. "Boston Is Bustin' Out All Over," *Theatre Arts*. XLIII: 8 (August, 1959), pp. 10-13.

_____. "The Brattle Paid Its Way—No Matter What," *Theatre Arts*. XXXVI: 6 (June, 1952), pp. 31, 88ff.

_____. "Death of a Playhouse," *Theatre Arts*. XLI: 10 (October, 1957), pp. 25-27, 90 ff.

_____. "Region 11," *Theatre Arts*. XXXIV: 8 (August, 1950), pp. 62-66.

_____. "Theater in Boston, 1792-1975," *Boston University Journal*. 23: 1 (Winter, 1975), pp. 3-11.

_____. "Theatre, USA: Boston," *Theatre Arts*. XLIV: 5 (May, 1960), pp. 53-56, 66 ff.

Picon, Molly. *So Laugh a Little*. New York: Messner, 1962.

Playfair, Giles. *Kean, the Life and Paradox of the Great Actor*. London: Reinhardt and Evans, 1950.

Quinn, Arthur Hobson. *History of the American Drama from the Civil War to the Present Day*. New York: Appleton-Century-Crofts, 1936.

Robbins, Phyllis. *Maude Adams, an Intimate Portrait*. New York: Putnam, 1956.

Ruggles, Eleanor. *Prince of Players: Edwin Booth*. New York: Norton, 1953.

Ryan, Kate. *Old Boston Museum Days*. Boston: Little, Brown, 1915.

Skinner, Cornelia Otis. *Madame Sarah*. Boston: Houghton, Mifflin, 1966.

Skinner, Otis. *Footlights and Spotlights*. Indianapolis: Bobbs, Merrill, 1924.

Stagg, Jerry. *The Brothers Shubert*. New York: Random House, 1968.

Stebbins, Emma, ed. *Charlotte Cushman, Her Letters and Memories of Her Life*. New York: Blom, 1972.

Tompkins, Eugene. *History of the Boston Theatre, 1854-1901*. Boston: Houghton Mifflin, 1908.

Tucci, Douglass Shand. "The Boston Rialto: Playhouses, Concert Halls, and Movie Palaces." By the author for the City Conservation League, Boston, 1977.

Webster, Margaret. *Don't Put Your Daughter on the Stage*. New York: Knopf, 1972.

Whitehill, Walter Muir. *Boston, a Topographical History*. 2d ed. Cambridge, Mass.: Belknap Press of Harvard University Press, 1968.

Winsor, Justin. *Memorial History of Boston*. Boston: J. R. Osgood, 1880, 1881.

Woodruff, John. "America's Oldest Living Theater, the Howard Athenaeum," *Theatre Annual,* 1950, pp. 71-81.

Wright, Louis B. *Cultural Life of the American Colonies, 1607-1763.* New York: Harper, 1957.

Young, William C. "Famous American Playhouses, 1716-1899, and 1900-71," *Documents of American Theatre History.* Vols. 1 and 2. Chicago: American Library Association, 1973.

# INDEX